Facing Life As the Girl from Nima

Memoir of an African Immigrant

RELEASE PRESS

Mariam Elias

Facing Life As the Girl from Nima

Memoir of an African Immigrant

by Mariam Elias

ISBN: 978-1-913478-94-0

Published by Release Press

Table of Contents

AUTHOR'S NOTE

A lot of people think I have a perfect life. In this book, I decide to open up in a way that allows families I cannot reach to sit back and know that they are not alone. We are all on a journey of ups and downs.

I hope that *Facing Life As the Girl from Nima* will reach my African sisters in a way that they can relate to. I pray that it challenges my African brothers to be intentional and thoughtful towards their wives. I hope that it makes African parents conscious of their parenting.

Finally, I hope that it challenges the African Muslim youth to be confident Muslims regardless of their struggles.

I am facing life, the good and the bad.

Ready to face life? Join me on my discovery to self-awareness and self-contentment.

Sincerely,

Mariam Elias

November 3, 2021

"Will I ever see my home again? I do not know.

Will I ever see my father again? I do not know.

Will life ever be the same again? I do not know."

—Na'ima B. Robert, *Far from Home*

PROLOGUE

It was a cold morning in November 2008, in Vermont. This was a day after the American Presidential election. I had a long, fearful night of what the outcome would be. It had been weeks and weeks of anticipation from all. The world was watching, as America could potentially have the First Black President.

I woke up at 4 a.m., as usual, to get ready for the Fajr prayer. I was in the bathroom making *wudhoo'* when I heard footsteps outside. I got scared. *No one wakes up at this time in the house except me.* I was with my white host family at the time.

I opened the bathroom door slowly to peep at who it could be. It was my host mom. I was surprised. She was up early than usual. She was all dressed up and obviously upset. I got scared. I quickly performed *wudhoo'* so I could run to my room to avoid any commotion. I had so much fear inside.

Did the Black man win? Did Obama win the election? As I walked out of the bathroom and our eyes met, I said, "Good morning."

She quickly took her eyes off me with anger and frustration. She went down the stairs hitting the walls as she went. I was so worried, so I followed her slowly. I thought that I did something wrong.

She opened her mouth, and the words that came out shocked me to the core. "I cannot believe that Black man won. Obama won, and I am so angry. I am leaving for work and not having breakfast in this house."

My feet could not carry me. I ran back to my room and started crying. This family hated Obama a lot. *Now that he won, they are angry. How do I react so they do not think I am like Obama?*

Life after that day was not the same. I did not feel welcome. I felt hated. They gave me a different plate and cup. I was told not to touch any white plate in the house. No one wanted to see me or talk to me. I felt so unwanted.

I cried myself to sleep for days. I tried to do every house chore in the house just so they could be happy with me. Nothing I did was enough. I started hating myself. I wanted to go back home to Ghana so badly. I missed my family. I missed my people. This place felt like prison. I started counting the days until my exchange program would end so I could go back to Ghana. I longed for home. I longed for Ghana. I longed for Africa.

Finally, I returned home to Ghana after a year. However, Ghana was not my home anymore. I was not welcomed. People had moved on without me. My friends had new friends. I was just "the girl who came back from America." Some family members were questioning when I would return to America.

Anywhere I'd go, I was somehow reminded that I acted different. The way I spoke and the way I behaved was different. I wanted to forget about America. So, just a few days after coming home, I started dressing in Ghanaian clothes. That was still not enough. Life hit me hard. Ghana was not my home anymore.

That was when I realized, *Home is where you feel comfortable.* I did not feel comfortable in Ghana anymore. I was now a traveler with an identity crisis. I have since been on a journey of ups and downs: betrayals, happiness, and disappointments.

I was born in the streets of Nima, Accra, Ghana, West Africa. Now, as a full-time wife, mother of three, and a student in New York City, life is not the same as before.

Life during the lockdown of the COVID-19 pandemic was the peak of my epiphany. I had to hit the "Reset" button to connect to what was most important-Family.

I had time to reflect, ponder and fix relationships. I saw a lot of families falling apart, and a lot of struggles in the African community. That was when I decided to leave a legacy. *What if I died now?* I thought. *What have I added to humanity? What have I done to help the African community?*

PART ONE

MY 'UNITED NATIONS' HOME IN GHANA

"I do not miss childhood, but I miss the way I took pleasure in small things, even as greater things crumbled. I could not control the world I was in, could not walk away from things or people or moments that hurt, but I took joy in the things that made me happy."

—Neil Gaiman, *The Ocean at the End of the Lane*

1

An Amazing Childhood

I was born in Nima, Accra, Ghana, West Africa. I had an amazing childhood. I am the second of three children. As a child, I remember laughing a lot and feeling loved. I grew up in a 'United Nations' home, as I liked to call it. Our house basically comprised of my grandfather and some of his children, male children to be precise, and their wives and children. So, you can imagine a square compound house with an old man and his sons and their wives and families. Growing up, I had about ten uncles in the house, four of them with their own families; wives, and children.

There was my dad, who had my mom, the best wife and mother I am still struggling to emulate. Till date, my mother adores my father in a way we cannot understand. Even when they disagreed, and you have her back, she will still find a way to defend him and make excuses for why he acted the way he did. My dad loved my mom, and my mom respected my dad. My dad knows he has a *keeper*.

My mom loves and cherishes my dad. I look at pictures of when they met and the story line of their pictures, and I go, *wow, this is beautiful*. My dad saved my mom's number on his phone as *Special*, and just seeing that any time on his phone makes me smile. My mom is my dad's die-hard fan. She has been his rock, his "Khadijah" and the one who keeps the home in check.

In this United Nations home, my younger uncle, my dad's stepbrother, married his wife and had a child before my dad married my mom. That means, my mom was the second woman of the house. However, till date, her qualities and management skills make people think that she was the first woman to enter our United Nations house.

My mom cooked and served everyone. My grandfather was always served first. He used to go back and forth between the village where his four wives lived and the city where his children and their families lived. Other children, uncles and aunts who were not living with us would show up on holidays, and that was the whole family's get-together time. We caught up with our cousins, laughed and ate with them. It was always a time we looked forward to as children.

There was also the wife of my father's senior brother who came to the house after my mother. She was our direct next-door neighbor. It was a fun house.

My dad was not around in my early childhood years, but I felt so loved by my uncles that his absence was not felt. When I turned five, my father came back from abroad, and it was strange at first. I remember asking my mother who he was. She said, "that's your father." In my mind, I thought, *Well, I do not need a father because I have a lot of fathers.* I did not know at that young age that the men that were there were my uncles. It took some weeks for me to open up to this new person and the dynamics of a father.

However, once I opened up to him, it was the best thing that ever happened to me. I had no one I loved more than my father at that time. He was my friend, my role model and the one who would buy me everything I wanted. Even at my young age, he valued my opinion. He knew I had something to offer humanity.

He would buy me cheese balls on the weekend and take me out to places with him. Surprisingly, my brother arrived a year later, and the dynamics changed. More attention was given to my brother, who was very cute and breathtaking. I loved him, but I felt he took most of the attention. Now as an adult, I understand he needed Mommy and everyone else more than I did. However, as a child, I did not know that.

My maternal grandparents were also involved in our lives. They lived less than a ten-minute walk away from us. We spent our long school breaks and vacations with them. My grandmother had so much love to give. There was always so many grandchildren there, but you could not tell who she loved the most. She loved us all very dearly. She recently passed away, and I am still trying to process it. May Allah grant her the highest status in Jannatul Firdaus, Ameen.

My grandfather on the other hand is a man of the Qur'an and discipline. He recited the Qur'an at least twice a day, after Fajr and Maghrib. He also did not let us get away with any misbehavior. The stories and wisdom we got from their sacred home is something I cannot place a price on. May Allah preserve him and grant him good health and long life, *Allahuma Ameen.*

Nima was a crazy place to live in. It is tough like the Bronx or South London. You must always be on edge to defend yourself and your loved ones. One must be strong. The environment was rough. There were a lot of fights, killing and mob justice. However, the sense of brotherhood and community was unmatched.

My older sister was quiet and reserved. She did not know how to fight. People would say things to us, and she would just run away or flee the scene. It irritated me a lot. I found out at a young age that I needed to stand up for myself, my sister, and my loved ones. That made me tough. That made me ready to fight. I beat up a lot of kids. I can hardly remember losing a fight to anyone. There were a couple of draws, but most were wins. I fought a lot because I had to.

2

Starting School

I attended Kanda International School (KIS), not Kanda School. I need to make this clarification because my parents sent us to private schools our whole lives. We went to the best schools they could afford. Kanda school is a "*Sito*" school (community school). It is notable for poor performance and naughty kids. However, there were a few kids that made it through. I attended Kanda International School, which was close to Faith Montessori School at Kanda. KIS was a private school and an amazing school. I had a good time there. I completed kindergarten through fifth grade (Class 5) there.

I remember those days when mom would buy me books and read some stories with us. My favorite books growing up were *Little Red*

Riding Hood and *The Gingerbread Man.* Daddy on the other hand would make sure we recited our Qur'an and said our prayers every day.

We attended weekend Islamic school, known as "*Makaranta*" (Madrasa), which started at 8 a.m. and closed at 2 p.m. Interestingly enough, we enjoyed them all. Mondays to Fridays were full school days, and weekends were for Makaranta. After Makaranta, I would come home and go places with Daddy or get to play with my friends while Daddy bought snacks for everyone. We lived in a poor neighborhood, but we were not poor. I felt rich because I did not lack anything growing up.

After Class 5, I moved to Aggrey Memorial School because my parents felt it was more disciplined than Kanda International School. My parents were always looking out for the best school that they could afford for us. My mom was always loved by the teachers.

After the school year ended, we would have a party called "Our Day". On this day, you'd wear your best outfit and bring your best meal in a basket filled with goodies. You'd have some food, juice, biscuits, candies, and gifts for your teachers. Mom always had an amazing gift for them on these days.

She also was in regular communication with the teachers during the school year, so whenever we misbehaved, she was informed, and we knew we were in trouble.

I was a good child in school. I was hardly in any trouble. I was either the office girl or class prefect. The class prefect basically helped the teacher in whatever capacity, such as writing names of talkative or naughty students to be punished by the teacher by the end of the day.

I was very shy and intelligent. I was a low-key smart student. I would rather answer in books but would hardly speak in class. I was terrified about public speaking. Just simply answering a question in class or adding a suggestion was difficult. I was timid. However, that changed when I moved to Aggrey Memorial School.

On my first day of school at Aggrey Memorial, I was very nervous because I'd heard that the students there were smarter and more disciplined than those at my old school. However, during break time, I joined the girls to play a game called Ampe.

Ampe is an African game where two sets of girls stand in line opposite from one another. You jump and clap while throwing your legs to match your opponent's. It starts with the leader of the line and her opponent, and it continues in that manner depending on who is winning. I joined them because I was good at it and also because it would help me make friends. I was the new student.

Sylvia, a skinny, tall, light-skinned girl approached me and said, "What is your surname?" Mind you, I just understood her as wanting to know my old sir's name. We refer to our teachers as Sir (male teacher) and Madam (female teacher). I instantly thought she mispronounced "sir's name" as "surname."

So, I ignorantly answered, "My sir's name is Sir Felix." She laughed pitifully at me. I thought to myself, *She was not in my old school, so why was she laughing? It is not like she knows Sir Felix.* I ignored her and continued with my Ampe.

The entire day in class was spent on people asking me what my surname was, and I answered all of them, "Sir Felix." It was only when I went home and asked my mom that I learned that *surname* meant *last name.* I felt so stupid.

The following day in school, some people tested me again, and this time I got it right. *Bam!* It was a slap in a lot of people's faces. They were shocked that I had figured it out.

I had fun at Aggrey Memorial School. I was liked by the teachers, and I was very good at English Comprehension, Composition, Dictation and Grammar. I had the honor to help my teacher mark some papers after our tests and exams. You know, I was one of the people with a beautiful handwriting and the student that would always do what the teacher asked.

3

Class Six

I was promoted to Class six (Grade 6) the following year. This was a change for me. We started the class with Ms. Asoumani, who was a skinny, tall lady who I thought was so full of herself. Later, I realized that she was just a confident woman who believed in herself. I admired her a lot and wanted to be like her, but at the same time, I thought she was too much. It was not long, however, before she had to leave.

I really do not remember what happened, but she left, and Mr. Dogbe took over. He was an interesting *Ewe* man. He had that thick Ewe accent with such big eyes that could scare the hell out of you even without saying a word.

I helped him mark, too, since he noticed I had a good handwriting. There was another student who was equally as good. It was Emily. I really learned a lot in this class and made a few enemies (haters) as well. You know that meanness among students where they want to push you down because you are soaring high?

There was a close friend I had called Doreen. Her dress and appearance were always spotless. She was very calm, and just being in her presence made me happy. I was the shy type in school. You could only get me talking during play time with my friends or any dancing activity. I was a good dancer, something my parents did not know. I would join any cultural display and dance event in school. Doreen was a beautiful soul. I often wonder where she is now.

I hated Ga/Twi (Ghanaian dialects) classes. This was the only time in school where I hated learning. Instead of choosing Twi, since you had the option of choosing, I chose Ga because Doreen was in Ga class, and she was my closest friend.

I was quite a follower at that stage in life. Ga was always very difficult for me. It got to a point where the teacher realized Doreen had been helping me quite a lot, so he separated us during his class time. My life was miserable afterwards. I only did well in homework since my mom helped me at home.

When it came to classwork, it was horrible. It was that one class that spoiled my report card. Every other class was an 80+ average, except Ga, which was mostly around 50 or 60% maximum.

Mr. Asante was the headmaster at Aggrey Memorial at the time. He knew my performance. I was the office girl, which meant I organized textbooks for different classes and put them in their respective cubicles in the main office for teachers. I made sure all tests and assignments were submitted and handed to the teachers on time. In addition, I did any additional job the class teacher assigned me to do, like taking attendance and writing the names of "Talkative" sometimes.

It was a good time in my life. I loved writing, so I wanted to be a journalist. It was the only time I was free to express myself without being judged.

I was judged a lot at home. Because of the nature of the house, everyone had something to say about everything I did. My uncles and their wives were always comparing us to their kids. There was this unhealthy competition among the children and an indirect competition among our parents as well. School gave me a safe space and took me out of the spotlight.

I graduated and completed Class six and was about to move to Junior Secondary school when my family heard about Ghana Lebanon Islamic Secondary School (GLISS). This was the first private Islamic school in Accra. It was a new school for Muslims.

My dad was so excited about it since we've had a series of religious conflicts in the schools we'd been attending. We were forced to take part in "Worship," which was basically dancing and singing and "speaking in tongues." That was not the difficult part, however.

The hardest part was having to memorize a biblical verse every Wednesday and sharing it with the class, with the moral of the story as well. If you came to class without a Bible, you were lashed (hit with a cane) for that.

At one end, we had a family that was religious and would dress us modestly from the house, but we had to take off our hijabs (head scarfs) when we got close to the school or at the school gate because they were not allowed.

Sometimes, there were random searches of school bags (backpacks), and when any religious garment was seen in it, you were lashed for it. Sometimes, it would be taken away from you and never returned. Just the thought of going to a school where I could cover fully made me excited. However, I had a whole community at Aggrey Memorial.

When we were not in school, we played in the neighborhood. We wrestled, played Ampe and judged a lot of cases in our little court room that we made. We had a lot of fun.

4

GLISS AND HIJAB

As a child, I could hear my dad making different phone calls inquiring about the school, and I was excited but anxious at the same time. He finally got the application and sat us down after dinner one night and said, "You will be going to this school for Secondary School." I remember our longest school vacation (Summer break) was over, and school had resumed sometime in August of 2003.

We still attended Aggrey Memorial as Daddy was finalizing the application for GLISS (Ghana Lebanon Islamic Secondary School). We started informing our friends that we would be going to a new school. Word reached our headmaster Mr. Asante, and he called me to confirm. I was so sad. I just nodded without a word. He said he will speak to my mom.

Since my mom was very present in our lives, she was active in whatever we did in school, so all the teachers and headmasters knew her in the schools we attended. He contacted my mom and she made it look like it was our dad's decision because it was hard for her as well.

Mr. Asante was not satisfied and decided to come to our home, unannounced, just to put my parents on the spot. He did, and they had a very emotional talk. He left our home very sad that night. You could tell he did not get his way, but he wished us well.

Daddy told us we would be attending GLISS, and GLISS it was.

My first day was amazing. It was memorable. I remember I wore a long sleeve top and skirt. The atmosphere was different. Seeing every girl in a headscarf (hijab) was beautiful and surreal. I was like, *Wow!* It is so beautiful to be surrounded by people who share the same belief as you and understand why you are the way you are.

The nerve-wracking aspect was being with rich Lebanese and white kids who would buy Coca-Cola and drink it like three times a day during a typical school day. They would buy the most expensive cookies and Lebanese dishes during lunch. I was in awe of that.

Remember, I come from an average family, so this was not normal for me. I was able to afford a decent lunch and few snacks here and there like candy bars or chocolate bars. I am grateful for that.

What I loved the most was being in class and challenging all these rich kids. It might seem like they have it together with their expensive outfits, lunches, and snacks but they were no match to some of us in class. Even though I was shy to raise my hands and speak in class, I always "aced" the quizzes and tests which made me noticeable after a short while by the teachers.

With time, the rich white kids started warming up to some of us because they needed help with homework. It felt good to have an upper hand against them in something. This is because they did not mix with the black kids at all. Even if you wanted to be friends with them by asking their names or saying "Salaam" in the hallway, they just rolled their eyes and walked away. Having them beg you for help with homework helped them learn what humility was all about.

After several weeks of coming to school with our individual outfits, the school finally got us uniforms. We started wearing uniforms to school and that made everyone more equal and comfortable in class and in school as well.

In my poor neighborhood, we were seen as the rich family sort of, so walking in those uniforms in the morning and seeing people point fingers at you and whisper to their kids that you attend that "expensive rich people's Muslim school at Circle" felt good and annoying at the same time. After a month or so, you'd think people would stop, but it took them over six months to get over it. It just brought more attention to us as a family.

I was particularly happy for my father because he put his salary on the line to support our education in a society where it was befitting for boys to further their education or go to the best of schools. His respect in the community heightened. However, it meant more pressure for me and my sister to be the best. All eyes were on us. What we said, how we behaved, who we'd hang around with, people were always watching. People would look at us when we were going to school, and sometimes you could hear them speaking among themselves. I did not like the attention, but there was nothing we could do about it.

I loved school. I was learning a lot about Islam. I was ten, and my love for the *deen* had heightened already. At Makaranta (*madrasa*), on the weekend, we were memorizing the Qur'an and learning about the *seerah (life story of the prophet).* At school, I was learning Arabic and Arabic Grammar. There were also Wednesday talks at the mosque, which used to be called, Worship and, later, Moral Training Sessions (MTS). We also had three days to celebrate *Eid.* During Ramadan, there was not a lot of quizzes, tests, and exams. The teachers were understanding and the leeway in Ramadan was the best.

Those sessions at MTS were amazing. Guest speakers from outside and mostly Muslims, would come and talk to us for about an hour and give us the opportunity to ask questions and they would answer them. It was a way for all of us to ask those questions we could not ask our parents or those questions one was afraid to ask verbally. There was a choice to write down the questions as well.

At GLISS, we had several sports too. There was basketball, volleyball, soccer, tennis, and Taekwondo. I joined the Taekwondo group. I learned so many self-defense skills. The Taekwondo master was impressed. He had no idea that I was a "Heavyweight Champion" in my neighborhood. Taekwondo replaced the fighting. I was happy.

I loved GLISS. I loved my teachers. I topped every quiz, test and exams. It was beautiful. Going to school was joyful. We all looked the same in our long green skirts and cream color blouses, with a white hijab (*khimaar*) on our heads. I loved being covered and at this point, the only time I took the hijab off my head was in the shower. Looking back, it's a bit unsettling honestly, as I would wear the hijab at home and in bed.

I freaked out whenever my dad saw me without hijab. I would quickly put it on when I saw him. I didn't even allow my siblings to see my hair. Then we learned about hijab, and I realized I'd misunderstood the part about not letting any guy or any male non-relative see your hair. For me, even my brother and dad were not supposed to see my hair. Before realizing my misinterpretation of hijab, it was tough. We would be watching TV sometimes or having a good chat together as a family and I'd be sweating beneath my hijab, but I feared taking it off.

I remember visiting my aunties and they would laugh at me because of how covered I was. I did not want anyone seeing any part of my body except my face and feet. I remember my hijab fell off one day when we went for a sleep over at my aunt's place. My cousins were there, and my unmarried aunties were there too. My aunt's husband was abroad, so it was a house full of my cousins and us with my younger aunties. I woke up for Fajr and saw my hijab on the pillow next to me. I remembered watching TV with everyone. How did I get to the bed, I wondered? I put the hijab back on and quickly went to make *wudhoo'* before waking up the others.

After Fajr salah, they were all laughing. My younger aunt said they were happy to see my hair last night because my hijab fell off when I slept in the couch. I got so angry, but everyone else was laughing. I was scared. *Is Allah going to be angry with me for exposing my hair to people that are not my immediate relatives?* It haunted me for the entire day. For the rest of the stay, I made sure I tied my hijab very tight and went straight to bed when I was sleepy. I did not want a repeat of what happened last time.

Alhamdulillah! After suffering for about four months, acting foolishly with my false understanding of the hijab, Allah rescued me with a follow-up lecture at Worship. The speaker explained hijab into detail and made it clear that your brother and father can see your hair. That made so much sense. I was so relieved because it was hard. I had been fully covered indoors and outdoors. The only time I could breathe, in fact my hair could breathe, was during shower time. That was why I stayed so long in the shower. Everyone would get mad when I was in the shower. They would literally beg me to let them go in first when I made a move to take a shower before them. Now, you all know why.

I was growing into a strong Muslimah. I loved the combination of studies. Monday to Friday was filled with classes that any Junior Secondary School in Ghana had, but we had Arabic twice a week, Worship on Wednesdays, and prayed Jumu'ah every Friday, plus *Dhuhr* (mid-day prayer) and *'Asr* (afternoon prayer) every day in school. Weekends were Madrasa Day, where we study the Qur'an and Hadith and other disciplines in Islam such as Fiqh, Seerah, etc. There was no conflict in my head. This made me appreciate my dad's decision of moving us to an Islamic school.

5

YEAR TWO AND MR. M

First year ended, and I was the first in class. We moved to our second year. We had more new students since GLISS was now becoming popular, as the product from there spoke for itself. We were well behaved. It was as though the world was watching us. There was no private Islamic school in Accra then, and the fact that GLISS was the first and the students were well-mannered and had a strong command of the English language made people interested.

Second year was tough because now the competition was tighter. Students had moved from all the top schools and joined us. I was envied a lot. I was shy and quiet in class. However, I was unmatched on a test, quiz, or exam. I was shy and second guessed myself a lot.

Growing up in a compound house and being shut down a lot for being outspoken led me to become timid. To a certain extent, I was tough in the neighborhood. I will beat you up if you'd dare touch my sister or brother. However, there was this "me" that was quiet and shy in school. School was not in the neighborhood. It was a different and a calm atmosphere, so I presented the best version of myself there.

I had teachers asking me to speak up in class. I would just smile and be quiet. They would ask questions, and I would know most of the answers. I would tell others by whispering or writing it down on a paper and passing it to them to say it. I would hardly speak in class. I had to be put on the spot and pressured a lot to speak up. Our Pre-technical Skills teacher (whom I'll call Mr. M) after a few tests realized I scored amazing.

One time he asked me a question and shouted at me to speak up. He said, "You know the answers, but you do not want to share it with your friends. Why are you being greedy?" That hurt me a lot. I was not being greedy. I was just shy. There was a difference.

Nabiya, on the other hand, was this free-spirited outspoken girl. Mr. M liked her a lot. There was a part of me that really admired her. I wanted to be like that. But there was just this voice in my head that told me to be quiet any time I wanted to speak up. The voices from my house and the neighborhood haunted me a lot. I was always speaking in my head about classwork, homework, test, quizzes, and exams.

Mr. M's love for Nabiya became so apparent, and he would always favor her. It became so apparent that the other girls had a meeting without her about reporting Mr. M to the authorities.

We had a suggestion box. This box was for us to voice out how we felt about any teacher, and we would not be in trouble, we were told. I was the Class prefect, and we needed someone to write what we all planned to say about Mr. M. No one wanted to volunteer. We all agreed we must do it, but who was going to write it down and put it in the suggestion box?

After going back and forth, the older girls decided I should do it. They said since I was the class prefect, it only made sense that I did it. *SubhanaAllah!* How foolish of me to agree to that. I wrote what we all wanted to say. In fact, they dictated the words to me, and I wrote what they said. The girls escorted me, and I put the note in the suggestion box.

We had Class meetings after Jumu'ah prayers every Friday. This was when the class teacher addressed any concerns, questions, or suggestions we might have about class. Friday came and our class teacher discussed the issue with us all. Some people were vocal and said he was always showing favoritism and that was not good. Nabiya was quiet and sad. We thought it ended there. Our class teacher promised us it would be addressed, and he would be spoken to.

Boy oh boy! Was it addressed! Mr. M came to class the following Monday like an angry lion. He was so mad that his words could not come out properly. He was looking at me angrily from the moment he entered the class. I knew this was not going to be good. He shouted at me, yelled at me, called me names, and I just wished the floor would open so I could bury myself.

The rest of the girls were silent and acted like they did not know what he was talking about. I turned and looked at the big girls who'd convinced me to write the note. I remember clearly writing each word as they dictated them to me. Now everyone was acting so innocent and leaving me to my fate.

I wished I could vanish. I was so hurt. I felt betrayed and backstabbed. I never enjoyed Mr. M's class after that incident. It was a disaster. He would assist everyone else and intentionally isolate me. It was as if I were invisible. The girls enjoyed it a lot, however.

It ultimately affected my grade in his class, which affected my overall grade. I could not challenge anything he did. He would intentionally not mark certain parts of my quiz. After the incident, I never got above a 65 in any of his exams. From this, I learned an important lesson in life: *Be careful of the friends that cheer you on. They may be the same ones that boo you at your downfall.*

The girls laughed at my discomfort in class and would chitchat with Nabiya like they were cool with her. They would laugh when the exam or test results come since they knew I was failing the class and could not fight back.

I made a lot of *du'aa*, and Allah saw me through. I made sure all the other subjects were a 90 and above to make up for Pre-Technical Skills. I ended up first place in the exam again. This time, they were all sad, and I was happy. I felt vindicated. We proceeded to the last term and I was first again...*Alhamdulillah.*

6

FINAL YEAR: JSS 3

After our long break, we entered our final year, JSS 3, and this was the year for our Basic Education Certificate Examination (BECE). Sadly, Mr. M remained a teacher of mine during that year. Every time I was in his class, I was nervous and anxious. To calm myself I was always reciting something from the Qur'an, like the three *Qul's* or *Ayatul Kursi*, or praying to Allah to not let Mr. M's eyes fall on me. I felt better when he ignored me.

Unfortunately, there were times when Mr. M would scream, insult me, or yell at me, and I felt horrible. I'd want the ground to open and swallow me. Being invisible in his class was better for me.

However, after seeing the sadness in my eyes and how the other teachers really cared for me whenever I entered the Staff Common

Room, Mr. M started coming around. I was so surprised. The main reason for his change, however, was that the school had promised the teachers an incentive based on how many students got 1 (the best score for each subject) in their courses. Getting a 1 was like getting an A in that subject.

Every teacher was now getting competitive and teaching with a lot of zeal and vigor. Mr. M came around so much that he even called me during break one time. He said there was a magazine offer that wanted a Muslim girl on the cover, and he wanted me to be on the cover of that magazine. I was not too comfortable about that. I wanted to go home and ask my parents first. However, he was asking me to take the picture right then during second break (prayer time) and said, "We need to take it now." So, I agreed, though I didn't really feel like I had a choice.

Alhamdulillah, it was in my uniform. I posed for three shots, and he said an article would be written about me and the school. I thought, anything for GLISS was worth doing. I loved GLISS so much.

Before we realized it, the BECEs were a couple of weeks away, and the school took us to the exam center to familiarize ourselves with the place. Every teacher was very supportive, and they all wished us well. The exam lasted for a week. There were two papers per day, three hours each. You would write the first exam and take about an hour break and then come back to the same class or a different class to take the next exam, depending on the invigilators (those overseeing the exam).

The daily trip to the exam center was a bonding time for all of us. Reality started setting in when we parted ways after the last exam. We would all be going to Senior Secondary School (SSS), and it might be in different schools.

On the last day of our BECE exam, people were confessing on the bus as we were driven to the exam center. Some asked for forgiveness for what they had done to me, but most did not.

We finished our exams and started jubilating by pouring water on our uniforms and using markers to write *Graduates* on them. It was a silly but fulfilling experience.

We came back to school and prayed our *Salaah* and parted ways. The results came out several months later and I had topped my class. I was the only one with an Aggregate 6, which was the top score every school wanted. However, the more people who got Aggregate 6, the better for the school. However, it was only me.

Alhamdulillah. I felt vindicated and joyful. All my teachers were so proud of me. They all called and thanked me. They advised me for the future. I told them not to worry since I would be attending GLISS, and they would still see me around even though I would be in the SSS building.

I loved GLISS, so I chose GLISS on my School Choice form. You had to choose three different schools. I chose GLISS as my number one choice, Achimota Secondary School as my number two choice, and GLISS again as my number three choice.

I did this so the examiners would know how much I loved GLISS. It did not matter anyway. I would be attending GLISS since it was a private school, and my dad was ready to continue paying the expensive school fees.

Mr. Abdul-Salam, my headmaster, called me and said I got offered Achimota Secondary School, which was like an Ivy League high school. Most of the Presidents of Ghana and Diplomats had attended that school. It was the dream school for most kids to attend Achimota. It had been my dream school when I was at Aggrey Memorial School. However, after attending GLISS and topping the BECE and helping my school's name come in the newspapers, I pondered, m*y school needs me. I need to be in GLISS. I cannot give all the hard work my teachers put into me to a different school to take the glory.*

So, I told the headmaster that I would turn down the offer since I wanted to attend GLISS. He urged me to think about it. "This is a once in a lifetime opportunity," he said. I could sense the hesitation in his voice and expression. "Well, go home, think about it and talk to your parents and then come back to me," he said.

I went home and discussed it with my parents. *May Allah bless my dad with Paradise, Ameen.* He looked at me and said, "I think you should continue at GLISS."

I said, "I think so too."

I decided to go to GLISS since it was the school that had my back and kept my faith in check. Not only did I get an excellent education, but I also got an inner and outer spiritual upbringing. That was the main reason that I wanted to continue at GLISS, and until today, I do not regret my decision at all. I would do it all over again. GLISS did not only give me an education. It nurtured me into loving Islam more and being a better person. I was happy with our decision.

Now, others around me were putting ideas into my head about how I would regret this decision. I thought to myself, *How can I leave GLISS and move to a school which makes you wear a sleeveless top and a short uniform?* The longest uniform went to the knee, and even then, your armpits were showing. Furthermore, you would have to cut your hair and shave your head like a boy and wear no hijab.

I've been covered fully for three years now, every day, and now I'll go to a school where I would be 'naked' five days in a week?

That did not sound good to me.

I was happy the next morning. I took my shower and got ready to head to GLISS. I got there cheerfully, and Mr. Abdul-Salam looked keenly at me to hear what I had decided. I said I would be continuing at GLISS. He seemed surprised and asked if I was forced to make that decision. I said, "No. I like it here."

Then I told him, "Yes, Achimota is a great and an amazing school with a lot of experience. We (GLISS) are new, and I know that. However, if I was able to get straight 1s in my BECE, then I can make it here as well in Senior Secondary School."

Mr. Abdul-salam smiled and wished me the best. "Well, here is the form for SSS," he said. "Fill it out and start your journey there. We know who you are. Please don't change."

I smiled back and thanked him.

I felt so good and happy as I walked out. I was reminiscing on all the awards I'd gotten in that JSS building. For all three years, I was the Overall Best Student. A year consisted of three terms, and I topped my final exams at the end of every term. I got the Most Disciplined Student Award and Best Arabic Student for Group B. These awards were given at the end of each term for the preceding term.

It was a beautiful and a joyful experience each time. All those memories brought smiles to my face. A voice told me I was making the right decision. I felt good and went home.

7

Senior Secondary School

I went to school one morning to meet the SSS Headmaster. I met with Mr. Mohammed Baba Alhassan, the headmaster of GLISS-SSS to submit my filled-out application form. He then asked me what I wanted to study. I said, "Business." He was not too impressed by that.

"What about Science?" he said. "With such good grades, you want to study Business?"

I said, "Yes."

He then asked what my parents wanted and suggested. "They also suggested Science," I said, "but I do not like science."

After going back and forth with him, he agreed to let me proceed with the application. I did, and I chose Business with Elective Math.

We had two options, Business with Cost Accounting or Business with Elective Math. I chose Business with Elective Math, which was the challenging class.

Unfortunately, when classes started, I mistakenly went to the wrong class. They were right next to each other. I entered the Cost Accounting class. It was an interesting class, but I did not like it because it was slow and not challenging. I then realized it was time for Cost Accounting and I was like, *Wait a minute! I am in the wrong class.*

That was when Zulaiha, the fairest girl in the class, asked me to please sit and wait for the class to end before moving. She and some other girls tried to convince me to stay, but I was not having it. I was polite and smiled about it. I spent almost the whole day there.

It was after the second break, which is after Dhuhr prayer, when I went to the other class. Just entering the Elective Math class was amazing. The feeling and the people there looked very serious. I wondered, *Wow! Did I bite off more than I could chew?*

I got a seat, and it was already time for the next lesson. I do not remember which lesson it was, but I was sure I was in the right class now. The next day, I was happy to go to the 'D' class. The girls from the C class saw me and tried convincing me to come back there. Some even took it personal and started making faces at me for not coming back there. I was like, *Wow! This is serious.* Anyway, I stayed in the D class, and it was indeed a Distinguished Class.

Toward the middle of my first term in Senior Secondary School, the Director of the School, Mr. Ali Soulah, called me and told me about a big event that would take place at the National Theatre. It was kind of an awards night for me and other students from other sister Lebanese schools. However, the condition was, I must show up with my parents only, no one else. I was excited about it.

I went home and informed my parents. It was on the weekend. We got ready that weekend, and I wore my nice long Eid dress. It was blue and yellow mixed with sparkles of long white dress. It was by far one of my favorite Eid outfits.

The lights were out, and it was a rainy day. I felt so bad leaving my siblings behind. How were they going to feel? Dad told them we would be right back, and we left. You could sense the pain in their eyes, so I decided I would make sure to bring them something from the feast.

National Theatre is a big center, and big things happen there. However, I just thought it would be half filled because they did not get any other center to do the program and that was why they chose the place. *SubhanaAllah!* We got there and I was gobsmacked. There were a lot of people. Everyone was dressed in their best.

We showed our invitation card at the entrance and went straight to our table as we were directed to. I was speechless. The place was flawless. There was a lot of food lined up like a buffet on several long tables. There was so much to drink and eat.

I felt happy that my parents were all smiles. I was honored to be the reason why we were there. We were then told to proceed to the auditorium for the program. We had to come back outside to the eating area afterwards.

There were so many Lebanese families. *SubhanaAllah!* That was the first time I saw so many of them at one place. Some of my classmates were there as well. We waved at one another and exchanged salaams. It was a sight to behold. I then saw some TV personnel and I was like, *This is bigger than I thought.*

After several opening statements from Big Tech people and the Lebanese Community President, the awards distribution started. They praised and thanked the leadership of GLISS and the Director, Mr. Ali Soualah, for the exceptional work done thus far. He was honored with an award. Now came the student awards.

Someone whispered to me and said I would have to go on stage to get my awards alone and then join my parents back at my seat for a group picture. I was so nervous. The big auditorium was filled to the brim.

What if I fall off stage out of stage fright? What if I do not walk properly and end up embarrassing my parents? What would some of my teachers say if I do not hold the award properly? I was so critical of myself. Before I could add more to the anxiety list, my name was mentioned as the Overall Best Student for the BECE exam with an Aggregate 6. The room was filled with applause from all corners, and I slowly got up. I looked down and carefully walked up the stairs to the stage.

The presenter was all smiles, and I received the award. There were additional gifts as well. I held onto it tight and started saying my *du'ad*'s as I walked back to my seat. I was in the spotlight, and I didn't like it. As I walked down the stairs to my seat, I could feel the flashes from different cameras on my face. I got embarrassed and looked down. I rushed quickly to my seat.

My parents were so proud. You could tell from their faces. I was glad to have put such a smile on their faces, *Alhamdulillah*.

Then the night was done, and we had to go eat. The food was good. I saw both headmasters with their families, and they congratulated me and my parents. So many people came to our table for pictures. I did not like the attention. I realized I had no bag to put some of the food for my siblings. It was then that I decided I would take some of the chicken tenders and put it in the napkins and quickly put it in my mom's handbag before people saw me.

A lady walked to our table and asked my parents if she could have a word with me. "My name is Fatima," she said with a thick Arab accent. Just call me "Aunty Fatima." She praised me and asked her kids to look up to me. She said she had an organization where she mentored girls my age.

I was fourteen at the time, and she said that was perfect. "Don't worry," she said. "I will come for you, and you will stay with me for the weekend. I will help you and pay for everything. I want to take you to Lebanon and teach you a lot."

My surprised face was met with a reassuring tap on my shoulder. "Don't worry," she said. "Your mom will know you are with Aunty Fatima."

Everything was planned and she said she had been helping other less endowed Lebanese girls and had been sponsoring their education in Ghana and Lebanon. She said she would be glad to do it for such a smart girl like myself.

I said, "Thank you." She asked for my parents' phone number, and I gave it to her. She said she would speak to my parents and my director and then we would start the process as soon as possible.

She wanted to take me to Lebanon in about two weeks' time. When she asked my home address, I said, "I live in Nima."

She abruptly stopped writing. "Huh" she said. "Where again?"

"Nima," I said. "I live in Nima, Alaska, Alaska Highway."

"Oh! I thought you live in a good place," she said. "Oh, okay." There was disappointment on her face as she closed the small address book she had. "I will call you," she said.

I knew it did not end well. Everything went well until I mentioned Nima. It was a gangster neighborhood. Most people that come from

Nima are tough. Some are thugs, and others are geniuses. Unfortunately, there is a bad perception that nothing good comes out of there. I felt let down. Nima is just one of the Zongos in Ghana. A Zongo is a densely populated Muslim dominated neighborhood. Nima is one of the famous Zongos. People have a lot of stereotypes about people from Nima, or the Zongos in general.

There is no proper sewage system for most houses. There is inadequate water, a basic need. Nima has many talents and skillful youth. However, there are less avenues and opportunities for them to explore their creativity. Lots of scholars and knowledgeable people in the field of Da'wah come from Nima. Most geniuses that break away from the marginalized system hold reputable positions in government, and some are entrepreneurs. However, there is still work to be done to help Nima develop to match the standard of most neighborhoods in Ghana.

However, I looked forward to Aunty Fatima's call in the coming days. Weeks passed, and we heard nothing. I even went to the director to ask him if a woman had called him, and he said no. I described her and told him what she'd told me. "If she wants to hear from you," he said, "she will call you."

The call never came.

My entire life up until then, I had never been ashamed to be from Nima. I loved Islam. I wanted to learn Arabic. I wanted to be in a place where Islam was practiced openly. I had started planning how life would be for me and how much Qur'an I would learn and how I would come back and teach my siblings. *All these dreams were crushed.* After several months passed, I had no choice but to move on.

8

THE QUR'AN COMPETITION

Life moved on. In the second term of the same year, I got a proposal from Mr. Wahab, one of my teachers from Junior Secondary School, about a Qur'an competition in Libya. I was shocked. I had been memorizing the Qur'an, and he knew about it. I hesitantly said, "I have not gone far."

"Think about it," he said. "Then let me know when you want me to test you."

I said, "Okay."

He tested me the following week and said I was good to go, but he advised, "Practice more because this is an international competition. People from all over the world will be coming."

I started practicing and informed my parents. They already had a relationship with Mr. Wahab because he was like my father in school. He really cared about me and my success in school.

I did not even have a passport, so we started the passport process. It was tedious and hectic. There were so many people we had to see and several days of back and forth. The passport office was a nightmare.

Alhamdulillah, we finally got it.

Not long after that, we were invited to the Libyan Embassy. I was interviewed and informed about the program. It is a fully funded program. I said, "*Alhamdulillah*."

My visa was approved, and the interviewer told me that I would be going with a chaperone since I was young. I was happy. "I will go with my mom then," I said.

"No," he said. "The chaperone must be someone from the organization."

I said, *Okay*. All this while, I thought it would be a female.

Everything was set, and the day for travel was quickly approaching. It was my first big travel. I had my pretty sparkly jacket and was dressed in all white. My grandma and my parents saw me off at the airport. It was there that I saw the representative from the organization. It was a man.

I felt disappointed. The excitement of going to a Muslim country outweighed my disappointment, so I quickly got over it. I checked in and quickly came out to say my final goodbyes. My grandma made *du'aa* for me and we hugged and said goodbye.

The airline was Afriqiyyah, and it was in Ramadan. I was going to be gone for a couple of weeks. The chaperone and I got on the plane. It was amazing. The ladies were so nice. It was my first time flying, and I was so nervous. The stewardess helped me with my seat belt, and I was all set. I said my *du'aa*'s and the plane took off. My tummy was rumbling and anxious. However, once the plane was in the air, it felt like I was in the living room.

It was nighttime. I couldn't sleep. I was so excited, I wanted to see everything. I saw a lot of amazing and scary things in the clouds. At some point, it looked like there was a round fire. I also saw something in the shape of a tree making *rukoo'*, as if bowing in prayer. I could see clouds beneath us and above us. Then I started getting scared, so I closed the window shade.

After a long flight, we arrived in Libya. We were received by a sister named Aisha. She was all smiles and black like me. It felt good. She spoke Arabic and English. I told her that I only spoke English and that brother Muhsin was my chaperone. He did not say much. Right as we got to the hotel, I saw Sister Aisha shaking hands with a man who was not related to her. It appeared to be one of the organizers. That shocked me a lot. *This is supposed to be a Muslim country,* I thought. *What is going on?*

I took my eyes off her and looked down. I was so ashamed. She asked us to wait in the lobby as they dressed and got our rooms ready. I saw other men coming and approaching her. She shook their hands and was laughing and talking freely with them. *But we are in Ramadan, so why are they shaking hands and laughing with each other like that?* I thought.

Other guests had come from other countries as well. The lobby started getting crowded. I saw a sister from Niger, and another from Nigeria. We exchanged salaams and someone told us that our rooms were ready. We went to our rooms. *Alhamdulillah*, I was happy we had separate rooms.

I settled in and Brother Muhsin knocked at my door a few minutes later. I opened the door, assuming he would speak to me at the entrance. He made his way into my room, and I did not like it. I was standing and he asked me to sit down. He made himself comfortable. I sat far away from him.

"I'm going to the restaurant to eat," he said.

"I'm fasting," I said.

"How?"

"The air hostess came to me before Fajr on the plane when I asked her what time Fajr is since she looked Muslim," I said. "She said, 'In about fifteen minutes,' and I asked her if it was okay to get something to fast with. She brought me some hot tea and bread, and I took my *suhoor*."

He said, "Oh okay."

"Yes, you were sleeping then," I said.

He proceeded to the restaurant, and I just kept admiring the place. I looked at my closet, then at the amazing bathroom and the TV on the wall with the variety of drinks in the fridge. The hotel was called El Mahari Hotel. It was a beautiful hotel. I showered and came downstairs to catch up with everybody.

It was a beautiful sight to behold. Brother Muhsin saw me and asked me to stay with him and said that we must go everywhere together. I felt awkward.

When it was time for iftar, I could finally eat. Everyone was sitting at the table with whomever they came with. I realized my friend from Nigeria had come with her husband. The other lady from Niger had come with a lady. I also saw a Kenyan girl with her dad. *Why did I have to come with a stranger?* It was uncomfortable.

Brother Muhsin and I sat facing each other as we ate our iftar meal. It was awkward. He was trying to make conversation while I was dead silent. I did not like that I had to be with him. It was nothing personal, but it just did not feel right. I wished I was there with a woman.

We finished eating, and I quickly rushed to the table with the girl from Niger and introduced myself. We started speaking Hausa. That made me so happy. After a day of hearing mostly Arabic and a little English all day, it was good to unwind with some Hausa.

She and I went together to pray 'Ishaa and Tarawih. We were led by a Malaysian Imam. He had such a beautiful voice. *SubhanaAllah!* There were so many of us, and some were sitting down during Tarawih. He really stretched it. His beautiful voice made it soothing. He had his *izaar* wrapped around his waist in his traditional Malay outfit.

After Tarawih, I said goodbye to my new friends and headed to my hotel room. Brother Muhsin saw me again and reminded me that I had to stay with him and stop doing things on my own. I smiled and went straight to my room.

He later came and knocked at my door. I opened it, and he said he had to test me on my memorization of the Qur'an because I would be called to be tested. He sat on the bed, and I sat far away from him on the chair. He started testing me, and it was so uncomfortable. The door was closed, and it was nighttime. I felt so uncomfortable.

Alhamdulillah, Allah intervened. There was a knock at the door, and a brother told us to come to a room to be tested. I got excited and we left my room to that room. I was told there was a lot of us, and the focus would be on the ones that have memorized the full Qur'an or half of the Qur'an. Those of us who had memorized a quarter would be tested last.

I was tested on five Surahs and I got four out of five right, *Alhamdulillah.* I was given a new prayer mat and a mild scented deodorant for women. The sister who was there was so nice and all smiles.

We left the room, and I ran straight to mine and said salaam to brother Muhsin and closed the door after me. The subsequent weeks were for growth and daily testing. There were people from all over the world: Tunisia, Oman, Indonesia, Malaysia, India, Yemen, Saudi Arabia, Niger, Ghana, Nigeria, Kenya, Ethiopia, Uganda, etc. It was such a sight to behold.

I saw firsthand how some people just partied at night in Ramadan, eating, drinking and chit chatting in the lobby. I did not expect that in a Muslim country. I was so shocked. The free mixing astonished me. Also, we had a visit by Dr. Gadaffi's daughter Aisha, and she was not in hijab. I learned from that experience that there are Muslims, and there are Arabs. There are Arab Muslims who understand the Qur'an directly but still do not observe the hijab.

We went to one of Gadhafi's dismantled houses where there was residue of shots everywhere. One of the contestants from Yemen and Oman recited the Qur'an so beautifully when we got there. It was so beautiful and heart soothing. I told myself I would take my Qur'an more seriously.

It was a couple of weeks of learning, testing and touring Libya. I loved it. Things were so affordable. I bought a lot of gifts for everyone.

I even said I would come back there for my wedding shopping *inshaaAllah*. I loved it. The elderly men were working. That was something I was not familiar with. They had their shops and were busy selling clothing, headscarves, thobes, khimars, jilbabs, niqabs, undergarments, etc. When it was prayer time, the shops would close, and people left to the masjid.

The only shocking thing was how expensive water was. A person from Libya would readily give you juice or soda, but water was expensive. I remember we got a liter of water to break our fast for five dinars, and that was a lot. I think that same money could buy 2-3 liters of soda or juice. I thought water was a necessity and hence should be affordable, but quite the opposite happened. That was very interesting for me.

When the competition was almost over and the rest of us were interviewed separately, I came third place, *Alhamdulillah*. I was given money, prayer mats, Qur'ans and some goodie bags. *MaashaaAllah*.

The next couple of days were spent shopping, and I did that with my Niger friends, Sister Aisha, and her younger sister Fatima. Brother Muhsin was very frustrated at this point. I just kept telling him I was hanging out with the sisters.

I disliked spending time with him. I had nothing against him, but he was not related to me. He could be someone's husband or brother. Since we were not related, it was awkward going around with him.

Muhsin wanted me to sit with him at the table for Iftar like the others did. The difference was, they were related. The organizations in their countries had made sure they'd come with their relatives. However, I did not get that luxury. I had to travel with someone I did not know, in fact, someone I'd just met at the airport. Now somehow, I should spend the weeks with him. Like how?

Anyway, there were two sisters that amazed me immensely during this trip. There was the sister from Oman who was in full niqab and *jilbaab*. She came to the restroom one day to perform *wudhoo'* and took off her niqab. *SubhanaAllah!* I could not count how many pieces of gold jewelry she had on. Her entire neck was covered with gold, *maashaaAllah*.

She had bangles and bracelets under her *jilbaab*. The entire time I could not take my eyes off her. May Allah forgive me. I don't remember if I paid attention to my *wudhoo'*. I was so shocked because my mom sells gold jewelry, and I see how sisters come and buy a little gold to wear on Eid day, a day which they felt free to abandon full hijab because they want people to see the jewelry.

This lady had way more than what people buy from my mom, but she covered it under her *jilbaab* and niqab. I told myself, *One day, I will dress like this InshaaAllah!* I was so impressed. I called my mom and told her about it.

I met another shy sister like me. Her name was Taqwa from Tunisia. She had a necklace made for her with her name on it. She always had it on top of her Abaya. She was always in either her blue or black Abaya. She walked looking down, very shy and modest. I liked her a lot. I could not speak Arabic apart from the basic greetings, so we could not speak much. We just smiled and exchanged salaams any time we crossed paths in the lobby, auditorium, or restaurant.

On the day before we left, I saw her and told her I loved her name. I said, "One day, I will have a daughter and I will name her Taqwa *inshaaAllah*." She smiled and said, "*Inshaa Allah*."

Brother Muhsin became very angry. He asked me if I had called my family to come pick me up from the airport. I said, "Yes, I called them earlier."

He said, "All right."

At this point, he got used to me talking to him in front of my hotel room door. I did not want to welcome him inside anymore. It did not feel right.

When the day to leave arrived, I realized I had some bills at the reception which I did not understand. They explained to Brother Muhsin that I had ordered *suhoor* twice in the hotel room.

"Yes," I said. "But the organizers told us that it was okay to order from our rooms if we felt too tired to come downstairs to the restaurant for *suhoor*."

They said they were not updated on that. Brother Muhsin kindly asked them to wait. I gathered my remaining money and was ready to pay when he showed up with one of the organizers who paid it on my behalf. I was so grateful and thanked him.

We left to the airport, and I said goodbye to my friends from Niger and Nigeria. I got on the plane and Brother Muhsin did not sit next to me. I was kind of happy but worried at the same time. He had a lot of anger and disgust on his face. I did not know what that meant. I sat by myself. I opened the window shade when and how I wanted and did not feel the need to be extra careful with how I sat or acted.

We arrived at the Kotoka Airport at nighttime. After we got our luggage, Brother Muhsin left. He just walked away after making some phone calls. He did not even look in my direction. I was like, *Wow! He did not even wait for me to leave first. How can he leave me here by myself? What if something happened to me?*

Just then, a feeling of strength came over me, and I told myself, *I got this.* The guards around the baggage area left and it was quiet. I walked and got out all by myself, quietly reciting *Ayatul Kursi* and *Suratul Ikhlas* from the Qur'an. I was anxiously waiting for my family, who finally arrived after what seemed like forever.

They worriedly asked me where Muhsin was. I said, "He left."

My mom was shocked. "What? He left you here by yourself and left? What did you do to him?" This was so like my mom. The de facto was, I did something wrong so that is why he left (in her head of course).

The ride home was full of joy and excitement. We got home and I greeted everyone and took a shower. The following days were filled with stories of Libya after 'Ishaa prayers every night. It was beautiful. Some people would sit, others lay on mats while some would stand just to hear me narrate the wonderful memories I had in Libya.

My mom still could not believe I did not do anything to Muhsin. She said, "We should go thank the organizers at the Libyan Embassy and show them the gifts you got."

We went there and did just that. Muhsin came and said salaam to my mom. My mom brought up the airport situation, but he shyly skipped over it by saying he forgot. Now, my mom was satisfied that I did not do anything to the guy. Somehow, I scare people, I guess.

I came to school after a week of relaxation. I wore my new Libyan school bag and shoes. My new name was "Libyan Borga" (traveler to Libya). I did not like it but got used to it with time. Life continued as usual, and exams approached very quickly. I quickly caught up with everyone else and ended up topping the class, *Alhamdulillah.*

9

Dreams of America

During the middle of the third term in the first year, I heard about an exam that people could take to go to the United States. I read about it in the *Junior Graphic*, a newspaper for youngsters. I didn't think much of it. I saw it on a Friday and the exam was the next day, on Saturday, at Oreilly Senior Secondary School. I just thought it was one of those ads where people want to go to America so badly.

Luckily for me, that evening after a program on TV, there was a quick ad about the exam. That was when I talked to my mom about hearing about it in school. My mom suggested I give it a try.

The next day was Saturday, and as usual, I was getting ready for Makaranta (Madrasa). My mom said, "What about the exam?"

"Well, I don't think I'm ready," I said.

She said, "Just give it a try."

I went with a pen, pencil, and a ruler. I remember it so well. I was wearing my pink flowered long dress to my knees with my loose pants and flowy hijab to my shoulders. I had a loose blue bag with just a pen, pencil, and a ruler with a torn eraser in the corner of the bag. I got to the center and was blown away.

I saw students from Achimota Secondary school neatly dressed in their uniforms and holding big textbooks and studying. That was when it hit me hard that this was real. I was like, *Oh God! I looked so unprepared.* I didn't even know anything else about the exam. I had to get a spot to sit to save my shaking legs from falling off.

There were over one hundred students. There were students from Oreilly School itself, Labone, Achimota and some other schools. Almost everyone had a mathematical set, a bag filled with books or a notepad, and they were reviewing some lessons or looking seriously into a book, trying to memorize and remember the lessons. I had none of these. I had only a pen, pencil, and a ruler, oh, and the chopped tired eraser, of course.

I had to sit back and take a few breaths just to make sense of everything that was going on. I managed to keep a smile on my face even though I was dying inside.

After about thirty minutes, we saw some volunteers show up who started preparing the classrooms for the test. It became very real now.

Now, I instantly remembered that I needed God's intervention because I was just not ready. We were separated into groups, and I was lucky to be among the first batch of students. Unfortunately for me, I was mixed with students from Achimota School. These are students I felt were full of themselves, and Achimota is the school I got into but chose not to attend.

We entered the exam room and took our seats. You had to just bring your pens, pencils, mathematical set, and calculator. I had no mathematical set or calculator. I remember the exam had three sections: English, Math and Social Studies. I think it was a three-hour exam.

Well, the English part was not a problem. That was easy and straightforward for me, as was the Social Studies part. However, the Math part was difficult for me, as there was no way you could go through all those questions without a calculator. I was so nervous and sweating.

The invigilators did not look friendly. I was fidgeting and finally got the courage to ask for a calculator. I was not surprised at the reply at all. The invigilator told me to wait until someone finishes the exam and there is still time to give me their calculator.

You should see the faces of those Achimota girls, looking at me like *You can't be serious* or *Where did you think you were going to?* I felt sorry for myself. I used all the math techniques I knew to answer the questions to the best of my ability. I used the remaining time to go over the other parts of the exam. I was done in an hour and fifteen minutes. Now, I just needed a calculator to cross check the remaining parts of the math section which involved some complex calculations.

Luckily for me, finally, a girl in front of me finished and passed me her calculator quietly without the invigilator noticing. I quickly cross checked my math work and fixed what I had to fix. After fifteen minutes of cross-examination, I was convinced that I was ready to submit. I quietly tapped the girl and gave her back her calculator.

I said my *du'aa* and got up to submit my paper. I was told to sit down and raise my hand and then one of the invigilators would come for my work. I did that and left the room. I was relieved and happy to go home after such a dramatic day. I got home and had to eat a good lunch. I think it was beans and plantain.

"How did it go?" my mom asked.

"Okay," I said. I did not give details because I was not ready to narrate everything. Later that day after Maghrib, when the family all sat down to watch the evening news, I remember bringing it up then. I narrated everything to my family in the briefest way I could. I did not have much hope afterwards. I was like, *With that number of students, I do not think I will make it, but I tried at least.*

Days went by, and I forgot about it. I did not make much of it. Then weeks after the exam, my dad got a phone call and was told that I passed the test and should be ready for an interview. They gave him directions to the AFS (American Field Services) office at Adabraka, Accra, Ghana. My dad said he would bring me for the interview.

Before this interview, and in fact, before the phone call, one volunteer whom I'll call Mr. A came over to my school to speak with me. He said the process was biased against Muslims, and he wanted to help me pass. He said he could maneuver his way since he thinks I passed the test but there were too many people. He gave me his phone number to give to my parents to call him. He said we must pay him. I did not feel comfortable about it at all.

I thought, *If I passed the test, why should I have to pay someone to help my name show up to the top?* My dad called him, and they had a talk. Thankfully, we refused his offer when he asked for some money to help us out. Not long after this encounter, I was called and informed that I had passed the test. You see, it means he was lying all along.

This time around, we had more communication between AFS and myself through my contact person, my dad. I started reading about the United States. I was not as nervous as I was before.

When I went for the interview, there were about fifty of us there. My name was called, and I met a panel of about four to six people who were all asking things about America and current affairs around the world.

I don't remember what it was, but Mr. Robert Asante asked me about a recent event which I watched on the news the day before. I also remember Aunt Aisha smiling and looking at me as I answered the questions. I was among the top people that passed with distinction, I was told. That boosted my confidence.

Mr. Robert, however, was very concerned about my dress (full hijab) and asked if I would dress like that in America. He said, "Well, we are here. You are going to come back and change. I can tell you that for a fact because we have seen a lot who start like this and come back with their skin showing."

I laughed it off because I knew who I was and what I stood for. Aunt Aisha appreciated my conviction and smiled throughout the interview. That gave me a good feeling.

I answered the rest of the questions, and I was told I would hear from them. Some days later, I was informed I had passed the interview and was now moving to the next stage.

We then had a few orientations where we met with the other finalists as well. We were all asked to make a sketch showing the direction to our houses. I remember thinking, *What are they going to do with this?*

Though I was getting closer to the opportunity to go to the United States, it still felt too hard to believe. *How can someone just take you to America to live for free for a long time?* my curious brain wondered.

I did not hear from AFS for a couple of weeks, so I thought I did not make it to the next stage. Remember, I hadn't believed it would happen anyway.

10

Dreams Becoming Reality

We were at home one evening watching the evening news on TV3 (a famous Ghanaian TV Channel) when my dad received a phone call. I overheard him responding "Yes, I am the one…Oh okay, let us come and get you." He hung up and said, "Mr. Djaba is here to interview you."

I asked, "Djaba? Who is that?"

Dad went out and I could hear him welcoming someone. *Oh,* I thought, *it's the old bald man I saw at the orientation who had a foreign accent.*

Djaba came into our living room and greeted us. My mom welcomed him to have a seat. It was quite a moment. I was nervous and anxious at the same time. I was thinking he came in person to tell me that I did not qualify.

He asked of my parents' names and my siblings. My dad was surprised at how Djaba came to our house.

"Who gave you the directions to our house?" my dad asked.

"She drew the map on the test we gave them and that was what I used to come here," Djaba said.

Now, the sketch we'd made that day made sense.

Djaba interviewed my parents in front of me, but I could not say a word. *Alhamdulillah*, they answered exactly how I'd answered on the page after the test and at previous interviews.

My parents were asked about curfew, homework, house chores, members of the family, and so on. Then Djaba shook my dad's hands and left. He thanked my mother also. My dad saw him off and came back to join us all at the table in the living room.

I was sharing with them how I answered those same questions during the initial interview and on the test as well. I was glad that I was truthful, so everything worked out. It was surreal and unbelievable still. I still did not think I would make it.

Weeks later, my father was contacted and was told I would have to come for a one-week orientation at Ghana Hostels (Legon Hostel). I was nervous. I had never camped with others before.

I spoke with my headmaster, and he gave me permission to go. I did not know if my teachers were aware, but my amazing headmaster,

Mr. Baba Alhassan said he would handle it. That man loved me like a daughter. *May Allah have mercy on his beloved soul. Ameen.*

I packed for a week's stay. I remember I wore a pink and a white striped long dress to my knee with my loose black pants (trousers) and a white hijab, with a black and a white half shoe. I was trendy. I loved matching colors like that.

We met at the AFS office in Adabraka. The other finalists also joined. Some stood out while others were introverted. Some just came there and started chatting with everyone else. I was one of the earliest there, of course, kind courtesy of my dad. "Being on time means being late," he often said. So, he was early for everything.

Everyone else came and met me, so it was easy to just respond to their greetings and conversations.

I liked Rafa a lot because she had her hijab on like me. It fully covered her head and neck, and her clothes were decent too. Our parents exchanged numbers and we became friends from there. There was also Fati and then Jamila. *Oh man! Those were some good times.*

As everyone gathered, we left around 4:30 p.m. and got to Legon Hostel at almost 6:00, Maghrib time. We were asked to choose our roommates, four people per room. I instantly grabbed onto Rafa and Fati and then Jamila joined in. After we had settled in and were happy with our arrangements, Anastasia was made to join us. I think Rafa was taken to a different room.

Now, I was on the upper bed and Fati was at the bottom. Anastasia was at the bottom of the other bed and Jamila was at the top. The three girls were very comfortable changing their clothes in front of all of us. I was shy and would look away, as they were fully naked changing their clothes.

I ran to the bathroom and changed. They saw me as strange, and I thought they were strange for not feeling shy and letting loose like that. They would say, "You are not in a boarding school, that is why you act like that." I would just smile.

I could not even let them see my hair. I would sleep with my hijab on in long loose clothes. They would laugh and make jokes throughout the night. I would tiptoe and wake up at dawn to make *wudhoo'* before waking Fati up to join me. Rafa would stop by our room, and we would all pray together. It was beautiful. Anastasia, who was not Muslim and so full of herself, would just stare at us and smile.

Anastasia was beautiful, confident, and flawless. She got along with everyone, and her confidence made her enviable. I was like her inside. I liked and envied her at the same time. I liked her personality, but I was enviable of her confidence because she got along with everyone and all the AFS staff seemed to like her.

Interestingly, we were shocked to hear that she would not be going to the USA with us. There were some last-minute night talk and grapevine circulating the last days we spent there. Rumor had it that she was part of the "wait-list" just in case a finalist pulled out or changed their mind. Apparently, no one was withdrawing at this point.

Anastasia looked devastated on the day of our departure. She wore a sleeveless blue jean dress, from her shoulder to her knees. She seemed sober on that day, not the usual talkative, vocal, pretty Anastasia we all knew. It had been a long week filled with learning, making friends, homework, and intensive workshops about the journey ahead of us.

Our parents picked us up, and we all departed to our homes. I kept in touch with Rafa through my dad's phone since my dad and her dad used to call each other. You would think the struggle would end there, right? No! Now we were asked to do series of immunizations (Yellow Fever, HIV/AIDS, etc.). Akai Clinic was the Clinic that the US Embassy trusted, so all the tests were done there. I remember my parents just paying for me and my siblings' school fees and struggling to put a lot of money aside for all these series of tests. *Alhamdulillah*, we completed that.

It was the week before my second-year finals when the AFS staff, the agency in charge of the YES program in Ghana, called my parents and school to inform them of another pre-departure orientation for another week. At this point, I was so used to missing classes that it was nothing new anymore. I had missed so many classes due to appointments, last minutes paperwork at the AFS office, countless orientations, interviews, etc.

This pre-departure orientation was intense. I remember Dr. Ato Selby, the doctor, who was also an alumnus of one of the exchange programs, was now a medical doctor. He played some interesting health games with us. He checked our teeth and passed comments. He noticed me because I stood out. I was always in matching clothes, fully covered, and shy. I would not speak unless I was called upon. The atmosphere was too competitive for me. Everyone was trying to prove themselves. I was not ready for additional competition.

I already had friends competing with me in my class at school. I was not ready to compete with finalists on an exchange program to the USA. I was very laid back, shy, intelligent but reserved. I gave all the right answers but would never willingly speak until I was called upon or compelled to speak. We listened to speeches and lectures from past alumni, Embassy officials, and alumni of other exchange programs hosted by AFS who shared their European experiences as well. It was so much information that I started having second thoughts about going.

Within three days before the end of this orientation, we got a surprise. Our host families wrote to some of us. A picture of my host family was given to me, and I was so excited. They looked happy and lived in a house by themselves, something I was clearly not used to.

I came from a big compound house, with uncles and aunties, so many cousins, and everyone in your business. This looked like paradise to me. I was so happy. You could see the jealousy in the eyes of so many finalists who saw my info from my host family. A lot of them came to me to see it and were comparing it with what they got.

About one third of the group did not get their host family's information yet. They were told not to worry and that they would either get it a few days before we travel or when we get to Washington for our arrival orientation. Everything seemed to be working in my favor. A few people were happy for me, but the majority were jealous.

This orientation also ended. Not long after this orientation, we were getting ready to leave Ghana to pursue our "American dream." My mom bought me expensive suitcases (at least expensive at the time). It was GHS450 in 2008. I felt awful seeing all my family's savings going towards my bags, clothing and cultural items and artifacts to give as gifts to my host family upon arrival.

I started e-mailing my host sister, Heather. Heather seemed more excited about her permit than my coming there. Every e-mail had something about her permit in it. At the time, I did not know what it was. I thought it was an exam that she passed, but I did not know it was her learner's permit (driving) she meant. I supported her and shared with her photos of my family too. All this while, I was using my dad's e-mail. My dad suggested I should start using my own e-mail.

This was a big deal for me. I liked using my dad's e-mail since he could read the message before I sent it out and tell me what he thinks I should take out and what to leave in it.

The shopping was done. I had two big suitcases and a medium sized carry-on luggage and a backpack. Now, everything was so real. We were called to show up at our last orientation, a three-day orientation for last minute paperwork, getting our passports and our visas. Did I tell you how we got our visas? Oh, that happened at the orientation before this one.

For the first time, we had a very decent looking hotel. I forget the name because we got there at night from the hostel after we were all tired. The rooms smelled good, and the lighting was amazing. The air conditioning was excellent. The rooms had fridges in them with some water already in it. Now, it really looked like we were getting the "American treatment." This did not last long. It was just an overnight stay.

You could hear the program leaders discussing the amount of money they spent as we eavesdropped from the window. They wanted something cheaper. One of them said, "Oh well! It is just for the night, and they will go back to the hostel, so there is no big deal."

We did not sleep that night. We were in awe of the rooms, the curtains, the AC in the room, the bathroom and the fridge, the iron and the soap and shampoos in the bathroom. We were also nervous about our visa interview. We were told what to say but at the same time, we were told our questions might be different. This time, we were in our school uniforms. I was the only one from an Islamic school, so

I was the only one in Hijab, fully covered with my long sleeve blouse and a long skirt, dragging unto the floor.

Ms. Val gave me the looks when she saw me. "Hmm, are you going to wear that on your head? They will tell you to take it off."

I was offended. *Why should I take it off? It is part of my uniform.* I started getting uncomfortable. Mr. Emmanuel also started giving me the looks. So far, he was nice to me. This was his last batch being the head of the YES Program and Ms. Val was taking over. We were given butter bread and hard-boiled eggs for breakfast. We woke up and took a shower very early. This was not alien to us because it was around the time for Fajr, so the Muslim students were not too bothered. The others seemed to be troubled by it.

We left the guest house at 6:00 a.m. because it was a thirty-minute drive to the US embassy and our visa interview was at 7:00 a.m. while there were about thirty of us.

We finally got to the embassy early. The embassy was not opened yet. We were made to line up like people line up for iPhone on a Black Friday. It was as though the world was coming to an end. It was as if they were giving us "heaven." You could hear lots of shouting here and there for the lines to be straight and everyone not to fidget or talk. The embassy was finally opened.

To our dismay, there were about three nuns who came there, and I smiled. I saw that they were also going for an interview, and they had their hair covered. I thought to myself, *If the nuns will not be bothered, why should I?*

Poor me! I should have known I would be treated differently because I was a Muslim. We finally checked in after over an hour of waiting in line in the hot morning sun. They did their check-in procedures, and we proceeded to the waiting area for the interview. This was just the check-in at the front desk or reception.

I was now in fear, but I tried not to show it. Everyone else did not look like me. There were talks and comments being thrown at me from all corners about them refusing to give me the visa if I do not take off the hijab. I started getting angry by now, but I stayed silent.

It became a laughing matter. Mohammed whom I thought would support me since he was apparently the GMSA (Ghana Muslim Students' Association) president at his school joined the squad to make fun of me. Mind you, this was the same guy that wanted to befriend Fati on an intimate level, but she refused. Sensing we were her friends, he tried talking to us to talk to her, but we all refused. This was his way of getting back at me.

11

Hopes for a Visa

It was about four hours of waiting before we were called. It was lunch time, but before then, we were told to go get some pictures again. The guys were interested in seeing my hair and the girls were more intrigued as to whether I would take the hijab off for the visa application or not. I do not know why we took the picture only minutes before the interview.

I waited patiently for everyone to take theirs. I was the last one now and Ms. Val was shouting at me because apparently, we had a little time left to walk and get back to the embassy. I was nervous. I sat down and got in position to take the picture.

The guy asked, "Are you taking it with this?" He was pointing to my hijab.

I said, "Yes."

He said, "Aye, you think they will give you a visa with this?"

I thought, *Why not?* In fact, there were two nuns that took their photos before me. I was supposed to take it after my friends, but they were still lingering in the picture room, so I told the nuns to go first.

After my colleagues left and it was just me, the nuns and Ms. Val, I felt a little bit less pressured. The nuns were just told to show their ears and their pictures were taken. No one commented about their head cover. Now, it became a shouting match when it was my turn. The anger of me letting the nuns take their pictures before me, coupled with us running out of time, was now on display. Mr. Edmond was in the embassy overseeing the line and corresponding to Ms. Val, who was with us outside the embassy, trying to get us all ready and back to the embassy.

After a series of back and forth and people chuckling and telling me I would be refused a visa, I started crying. I took the big scarf off and left the inner one. Now my ears were showing so it should not be a problem. The photographer said he needed my full forehead, so I should push the scarf backwards a little.

Ms. Val screamed, "Why don't you just take it off?"

I answered, "But the nuns did not take it off."

And the response I got was, "But they are not Muslims. Ah, why are you a small girl giving us problems like that? Just take it off. Take the picture and let us go. Everyone else took it with no problem. We are spending more than ten minutes now trying to tell you to just take it off and let us get the picture and then you can put it back on."

Now, she even got louder. "Are you the only Muslim here? Didn't you see your colleagues taking their pictures without it? What at all do you want to prove?"

I was humiliated. Ms. Val was shouting, and the photographer was threatening that my visa would be denied if I covered my hair. He said he had been doing this for years and everyone takes it off. "Why are you, a small girl, giving us a hard time?"

I was flooded with tears at this point and missing my dad. He would have told me what to do at this point. But who was I to say I want to call my dad?

I took my hijab off and closed my eyes. I just turned fifteen a few days ago. I was not a child anymore, and I felt naked. *A strange man with a barking woman in a strange room, taking a picture of me without hijab, just to get a visa?* I almost said, *"No!"* Thoughts of all my mother's spending and expenses came to my mind. I could not do this to her now.

I heard the photographer laughing at this point, saying "*Shw333,* open your eyes. How can I take a picture with your eyes closed?"

I opened my eyes and told him to quickly take it. Those two flashes were the worst pictures I have ever taken. My privacy was intruded, just because of a visa to America.

We walked back to the embassy which was right there. I came and joined the long line of friends who were laughing and giggling. I knew they figured I finally took my hijab off to get the picture taken. I was so upset. I wanted to get out of there. I wanted the day to be over already.

Thankfully, after thirty minutes of waiting, we were called to four different windows. Each person's picture was put up at the window for confirmation since there were many of us. Also, sometimes the embassy staff could not pronounce the names properly, so the picture gave a confirmation of who was being called.

I was praying quietly that I would be the last to be called so no one sees my picture without hijab. So far, it was going as planned. Everybody else was called. Now, it was about five of us left. Took off guard, I was called, and Emmanuel, Frank and Mohammed were just standing by. They quickly peeped at the picture and started laughing. They ran back and were whispering to the others. I felt so hurt and naked. It was as though they saw me naked. I went straight up to the window and smiled sadly.

Mohammed was laughing with them. I thought he would tell them to stop and share with them the reason why we wear the hijab. Instead, he teased, saying, "Some of them cover because of their skin rash or certain marks they do not want others to see." I was so disappointed and hurt by his comment. After all, what did I expect from him? He never got the chance to be as close to us as he wanted.

The lady smiled back. She asked of my name and then the reason for travel and nodded as though she knew that was what I was going to say. She nodded and said, "See you soon."

I knew my visa was approved. I smiled happily and turned to take my seat when I saw and heard my friends laughing and giggling. It reminded me of what had just happened. I was quiet the rest of the day.

The day was done now. We were all set. We went back and got ready to go home and prepare for the big travel. We were all so excited. We came with our suitcases ready to embark upon a life changing journey.

12

Preparing to Travel

The night before our travel was so memorable. We ate, and our passports were given to us with our itinerary. We had to make sure we put a tag on our bags for identification. I remember my bag was unique, but Ms. Val told me I still needed a tag. Upon insistence and pressure from her, I tied my orange and gray hijab on my biggest suitcase, and the other had a name tag and a bright marker on it.

I could not sleep that night. There were butterflies in my stomach. I was dreaming of how life in America will be perfect, how my host family will love me, and how I will love them. *I will finally come out of my shell and be the outspoken Mariam I have always wanted to be.*

Longing for morning and not being able to sleep, I woke up for Fajr feeling exhausted. We were rushing to use the bathroom when we heard Ms. Val screaming at us in the hallway, "We are leaving by 5:00a.m.!"

It was already 4:36 a.m. Rafa, Fati, and I quickly prayed Fajr. We then hurriedly got dressed and started pulling our luggage out of our rooms and then headed downstairs to the long bus that was waiting to take us to the airport.

It was my first-time wearing jeans or trousers (pants) that was somewhat fitting. I was so uncomfortable. Up until then, I remember wearing jean pants only once, and I wore them with a long Pakistani outfit that slid down almost close to my ankle so you could only see the end of the jeans instead of all of them. This time, we were told we had to look smart and to be ready to run, to drag our luggage by ourselves, and to do a lot of climbing. So, everyone had to be in pants (trousers).

I wore a long, loose pink dress which flowed down from my shoulders to my knees. You could only see the jeans from my knee downwards. It was not stretchy or sticking to my body; however, I felt uncomfortable.

We finally got into our seats in the bus. Our luggage was hanging on top of the bus, some at the back. My tummy was rumbling out of fear and anxiety. I had this strange feeling that I might not make it to the plane. The ride to the airport was bumpy. Most people were excited. Some of us were quiet and reflective. I was looking out the window and enjoying my last view of the streets of Accra.

We finally made it to the airport. The plan was for our parents to meet us outside the airport and say their goodbyes before we left. It was now 6:45 a.m.

We got out of the bus, and each person took their suitcases out. We had to sit on our luggage or have it next to us while we waited for everyone to line up so we could say our final goodbyes and head to the entrance. Amos was selected as the leader of the group, to put everyone in check and make sure the group was together.

I kept looking at the parking lot to see if my parents would appear. There was no sign of them. I could not ask Ms. Val to use her phone because of her stoic nature. I was wondering if I would get to see them before leaving.

Finally, Rafa's parents showed up. Her mom was in full hijab from her head flowing down. I started smiling. I welcomed them, and they stopped right where Rafa and I were standing. I also met Rafa's siblings. We talked, and her mom gave us her final advice to be there for each other and come back better than we left.

Shortly after that, I saw my mother waving. I felt so relieved. It was like I did not need to use the restroom anymore. The urge left my stomach. I started feeling less anxious now that my mom was here. I welcomed her with a big smile, and she was so emotional.

I could tell my mom was sad. Her eyes were a little heavy, but she was trying hard to hold it together. By now, some time had passed, and we had to go check in. Dad was still looking for a spot to park his car.

We quickly headed to the entrance, and I kept looking back just to make sure that if I did not come out of that door again, I could see my mom a couple of times before leaving.

We went inside and checked in our suitcases and carry-on bags. I had my backpack and my green winter jacket on my arms. I was holding my passport and I-940 form. Fearing dropping the paperwork, I put it in the jacket and rushed back out to say my final goodbyes and hopefully see my dad.

I could hear Ms. Val screaming, "We do not have much time, so you should just head to the boarding room!"

I thought, "No way! You told us we would have some time to come out and say our final goodbyes to our families." I checked the board to make sure there was some time. I told Amos I would be right back.

I rushed out of that door like my life depended on it. From a distance, I saw my dad, mom, and sister. I started smiling. This time, I gave my mom a hug and I could see my dad's eyes getting emotional. He gave me his final words: "Be conscious of Allah and make the best of this experience."

Strangely, I had my yellow winter coat which I took out of my suitcase with the green one. I said, "One jacket will be enough, so I don't have too much stuff to hold."

Dad said, "You should go with the green." Then he took the yellow jacket.

After saying our goodbyes and duas, I left them sobbing with the green jacket in my arm. It was like a scene out of a movie. I did not want to go. I almost said I was not going. At the same time, I wanted to make them proud and get a "better life." I ran quickly as my jackets swayed between my arms and backpack bouncing behind me as I was looking at the quiet walkway to the entrance of the airport.

I got there and wanted to check in and hurry to the boarding room and join everyone else. It was now about thirty minutes or less to board the plane. I could not find my passport or my I-940. I was shaking and sweating. I searched both pockets of the green jacket.

I could see my friends from the other side of the aisle. They were waiting for me in the boarding area. Some were shaking their heads, and Rafa seemed concerned. It was then that the dream that I had about being left behind resurfaced in my mind. I started making dua and remembered that I had put the documents in the yellow jacket that I'd handed to my dad. Immediately, I started running back.

Amos and the others were asking, "Where are you going?" Ms. Val was screaming, "The plane will go and leave you!" Then she said to the others, "We can't wait for her, so you guys will have to go and leave her."

I ran like I never did before in my life. Allah bless my father! He always told us not to leave a person at the airport until we see the plane leaving in the sky. He was right there waiting with my mom and sister. He saw me running towards them and got worried. He started asking, "What happened?"

I was out of breath and pointing to the yellow jacket he was holding. Confused, he looked at it and looked at me. Now, I was right in front of them. I leaned on my sister and caught my breath. I said, "I do not have my passport and documents to travel, and I think it is in the yellow jacket."

Just then, he searched the jacket and found the passport and travel documents. I tossed the green jacket to him, grabbed the yellow jacket, and run like the speed of a cheetah towards the entrance. My dad looked on worriedly. I waved from the entrance and headed straight in.

I could not see anyone. There was no line and the lady at the check-in just shook her head at me. I came and showed her my tickets, my visa and the I-1940. I was good this time. I then ran to the boarding area, and the rest of the crew were happy to see me. I just had to take a seat and soak everything in.

A voice told me, *This is a sign from Allah that you should not go on this trip*. Somehow, I ignored it and convinced myself that everything would be alright. This was my second time boarding a plane, so I was not that worried.

We boarded the plane, and it was such a sight to behold. Benedicta, who had never boarded a plane before, was acting silly like many others when the plane took a bumpy start. I was in my seat reminiscing on what had just happened minutes ago. I thought to myself, *What would have happened if my dad was not there? What would have happened if my family had left earlier?*

Everything made sense now. What my dad always said about waiting to see the plane in the sky before walking away when you see someone off at the airport made sense now. *What would have happened if they were not there?* I would have been left behind, of course.

It was a long twelve-hour flight to New York on Delta Airlines. We were served some yummy cheesy bread with several beverages in between.

I could not sleep. I was worried about my prayers. *How do I perform Salah?* I was shy to ask. I prayed in my seat and enjoyed the ride. Just when I wanted to get up and use the bathroom, I saw a long line at the bathroom door.

We were now almost at our destination. The pilot made the announcement. I stood up and headed straight to the bathroom. I brushed my teeth and made *wudhoo'*. There was some slight turbulence, and I realized the plane was landing.

PART TWO

SEARCHING FOR HOME IN AMERICA

"I am from there. I am from here.

I am not there, and I am not here.

I have two names, which meet and part,

and I have two languages.

I forget which of them I dream in."

— Mahmoud Darwish

13

From Nima to America

The airplane landed in New York (JFK airport), and people started clapping. That was strange to me. Well, I sighed a huge relief and walked out of the bathroom. I said, "*Alhamdulillah*."

We got out of the plane and started searching for our luggage at the baggage claim area. To our dismay, we all did not find our luggage. We had to head to the hotel for our arrival orientation, so Amos, the group leader, called and notified the staff in New York. We were told to head to the hotel, and it would be sorted out.

I needed to take a shower badly. *What am I going to be wearing?* It was morning, so we headed to our hotel. We were welcomed, and it was such a surreal moment. We met all sorts of people from all over the world: Kenya, Uganda, Rwanda, Indonesia, Pakistan, Uzbekistan,

Kazahstan, Saudi Arabia, India, Malaysia, Thailand, Philippines, etc. It was a sight to behold.

We settled in and were later split into groups to have a tour of Washington D.C. We visited the Lincoln Memorial, the Washington Monument, and other tourist sites in D.C.

Day two came, and our luggage was still not found, so we had to wear the same outfits from the day before. We were mixed in our hotel rooms, so my roommates this time were not Ghanaians. I had two Indonesian roommates and one Thailand exchange student.

The Indonesian girl sensing my worry of repeating the same clothes gave me a dress to wear, *maashaaAllah*. I was so grateful. There were a lot of Indonesians. Everywhere you went around the Center (4H Center), you would see at least one Indonesian. They were generally nice and curious.

Our three-day orientation came to an end, and each of us had to continue our travel to our "home" state, where our host family lived. This was the toughest part. Reality set in very quickly, because all this while, we were still seeing one another in the hallway, at lunch, at dinner and during breaks from group activities. Now, we were each heading to our host state to start our exchange year adventure.

I could hardly eat anything. I wondered why they served us scrambled eggs every morning. It was as though my taste buds had vanished. Nothing made sense.

Our luggage was finally here, and we all changed and looked fresh. Some were more excited than others. We were separated based on the part of the U.S. that we were going to: Central, Western, Eastern, etc. I was in the New England group (New Hampshire, Vermont, Massachusetts, Connecticut, and Maine).

I did not like the group coordinator. He was an old stoic white man who did not seem to care much about how we were feeling. He was very straightforward and dismissive with his words. He gave us our itinerary and told us the times we were all boarding the plane and what not. He was cold.

I was with Ami in that group. She was a very hyper and loud Muslim girl. She seemed fearless and full of life. I liked the fact that she was free-spirited and open, but I did not like the fact that she was loud. I did not know we would be crossing paths again.

We headed for the airport and said goodbyes to one another. This was very sad. I was trying very hard to hold in my tears. Plus, I started getting hungry. It was 11:00 a.m. by now. I was hungry because I did not eat breakfast. Earlier, I had some oatmeal but could not eat it because I was nervous and anxious.

We got to the airport security, and I was stopped. I was the only Muslim in that group. Everyone else left, but they stopped me. They asked me if I had any electronics with me. I said, "No." They asked if I had any sharp objects with me. They asked if they could search my hair and if I had anything. I said, "No." Now, I was getting frustrated.

There were two men, and I was not going to let them check my hair, of course.

They asked again, “Do you have anything in your hair? Do you have any object under the scarf?” They asked as though I did not understand them the first time.

I said, “No!”

One of the security guards called for a female because they said they need to check me out and search me from head to toe. The look I’d given them prompted them to ask for a female guard for me.

She came and sheepishly said, “We need to pat you down.”

I said, “Okay.” She asked the same annoying questions the male security had asked. I said, “No.”

At this point, I saw way too many people coming and going like no one’s business.

“Why am I being humiliated like this? Everyone else is coming through and going to the next gate,” I said. “Why am I stuck here?”

The lady asked if I could take my hijab off for her to see my hair. I said, “No.” She asked if she could put her hands in my hair. I said, “Yes.”

At this point, I was not only tired of their nonsense, but I was getting worried that the plane would leave me behind. I did not see anyone else coming to the check-in area. *That might mean it is almost time to board.* I got agitated and started feeling sorry for myself.

After putting her hands in my hair, sideways through the hijab, the security guard patted my hair and took her hands out. She used the metal detector to touch my body and literally squeezed me from head to toe.

A white lady came and passed by. She just went through and paused to see me look so helpless and distressed. I started crying, but the TSA did not care.

"You can go now," they said.

I walked past them a little and had to proceed to the boarding gate.

The white lady said, "I am sorry for the way they treated you."

"Thank you," I said and continued walking. A voice came into my head and said, *"Do not board the plane. It is going to be a nightmare. This right here; the treatment you just received from the TSA should tell you what awaits you from the other side."*

I ignored the voice and proceeded. Still crying, I headed to the boarding gate and boarded the flight. This was domestic travel, so there were no double check-ins and procedures.

The whole time on that flight I was sobbing and wishing I was not there. It was a quick flight, about fifty minutes, I think.

Before I realized it, we were in Hartford, Connecticut.

14

Meeting My Host Family

After 30 mins of waiting, my host family arrived with a banner, "Welcome Mariam." It was beautiful. I smiled at them and went straight ahead. I am a hugger, so I wanted to hug them, but I was welcomed with a hand shake instead. I took it and continued smiling. I thought we were going straight to the car, but my host mom said she had to give another student a ride because her family was late and could not make it to the airport.

I wondered who it was. Not long! Here comes Ami walking towards us. She came with her loud self and said hi to them. My host mom hugged her. That seemed weird. I thought to myself, *I am your exchange student, but you are hugging her when you did not hug me?* I'd offered to hug, but it was shrugged off and replaced with a handshake.

My host mom made jokes with Ami and opened the door for her to enter first. I disliked it, and I disliked Ami instantly. It was one thing being loud and talkative, but now she was making me seem invisible. It was as though I was not there. All the attention and questioning went to her.

I was silent for about ten minutes into the car ride. Sensing my silence and looking through the driver's mirror, my host mom said, "Hey! See? The banner color is matching your pin?" She pointed to my hijab pin. I smiled for being noticed finally.

We finally took Ami to her house and headed home. I was relieved. *Finally, they are going to pay attention to me.* I was welcomed into a nice-looking house, just like in the picture. However, we were in the countryside. I was in Guilford, Vermont. The distance between the houses were like a ten or fifteen-minute walk. I saw a lot of trees and mountains. It was different from what I saw on TV.

Anyone outside America knows that America is portrayed in the TV like this flawless place, full of tall buildings and rich people. I was picturing a place like Manhattan or Times Square. *What is this place?* I wondered.

I was shown around the house and my room. I was so excited about my room. Growing up, I shared the room with my siblings. *Now I have my own room.* That was exciting. There was a big bed with a quilt and three teddies on it.

I changed, and we headed for the gas station to buy a calling card since I insisted that I wanted to call my parents to let them know that I'd arrived safely to the U.S. Mind you, it had been almost five days since we'd left Ghana, and they had not heard from me.

We headed to the gas station. It was quite a ride. We got there and asked for a calling card to Africa, but the guy said he did not have one for Africa. He had one for Central America. He showed us another gas station, and we went there.

We finally got a $10 international calling card. It was not only for Africa. It was for other places as well. We came home, and I was looking forward to finally hearing my parents' voices. We tried and tried for about three times, but we could not figure out how to use the card.

They were asking me how to do it. I was like, "I don't know." They looked at me like I was supposed to know how to make an international call.

After a few more tries, my dad answered. He was so excited. I spoke English because my host family were all there looking at me, and I did not want them to feel some type of way if I spoke in a language they did not understand. Daddy was so excited. He passed the phone around for me to say hi to the others, but my host mom started shouting that we can email each other since the phone company would charge them for us speaking.

That was confusing to me. My parents wanted to talk to them. I passed the phone to my host mom, and she said hi to them. My dad was thanking her and praying for her when she passed the phone to her husband and winked at him to hang up. After I looked shockingly at her, she repeated that the phone company would charge them for this call.

I thought to myself, *Didn't we load the calling card before making the call? Why would the phone company charge you then?* However, who was I to voice what I was thinking?

My host dad said hi and immediately hung up as his wife suggested.

It was an awkward dinner. They had hamburgers and a few things on the table. I remember the Imam in Washington D.C. telling us that we can just eat a chicken burger or a chicken sandwich, not hamburger, since ham is pork. I thought, *Why would they serve ham or pork when they know I am Muslim?*

My host dad passed the hamburger to me, but I smilingly refused. He smiled back. I don't remember what I had because I was so focused on watching each of them at the table munch into the "hamburger" and wondering why they would serve that on my first day with them.

The subsequent days with my host family were amazing. I was introduced to different dishes and family schedules. We went shopping together at Walmart.

I remembered my host mom telling me, "We wear sanitary napkins here. We do not put leaves." I thought, *Wait! What is she talking about?* She asked what we used back home since she saw the surprised face I had.

I said, "We use a pad." I then described it to her.

She said, "Well, the ones we have here have wings, and they hold your underwear." I got really confused. I was like, *What is she talking about?*

She asked which toothpaste we used at home as well. I said, "Pepsodent."

She said, "We don't have that here. We have good ones here, of course."

I felt insulted. I thought to myself, *Well, the one we have in Ghana is good too.*

We got to Walmart, and I was surprised at how big the store was. Now, I felt like I was in one of those American movies. It felt real that I was in America now. This was after an hour drive from where we lived. We bought some toothpaste, sanitary napkins, and groceries.

My host mom was so keen on showing me the toothpaste. "This is what we use to clean our teeth," she said.

"Yes, we have the same thing in Ghana," I said. "Also, we have *Always* pad too."

She kept saying, "But these have wings to hold." I kept quiet. She gave the sanitary napkins to her daughter who needed it.

Later, of course, I found out that they were the exact same ones I had back home.

15

STARTING SCHOOL IN AMERICA

Several days passed, and school was about to start. We got ready for registration and went to the school. I attended Brattleboro Union High School (BUHS). It was a big rural public school. It was nice and welcoming and quiet when we got there. There were so many whisperings and looks when we got there. I realized I would be a minority there because all I could see was white people.

However, I was in for a great shock. After we registered for my classes, we saw the Diversity class teacher in the hallway. Heather, my host sister, introduced me to him. He was nice and smiled. He said I would help him when school starts. "You will share your culture with us, right?" he asked. I shyly said, "Yes." I was still in the honeymoon stage at the time.

I loved exploring and would go anywhere and everywhere when called upon. I liked to go with my host mom to recycle used stuff and to throw out the garbage, to pick up Michael; my host brother from soccer practice, to buy gas, to get fruits, to get some maple syrup; etc. I liked seeing more and more of outside.

I could see and sense the jealousy in Heather's eyes. She would get mad sometimes if I went out with her mom and she opted not to go with us. I quickly realized that I did not want to be like Ami, so I had to change. I started laying back a bit, and Heather enjoyed her mom fully now. The jealousy was over before it got out of hand.

School was starting in a few days, so we shopped for some school supplies. I paid for them with my monthly stipend. We got a monthly stipend of $125 which I wanted to save to buy a laptop. However, I was asked to pay for my school supplies. I don't know why I thought my host mom would pay for me like she did for her own children.

Gradually, it started to click that she would always refer to me as her exchange student wherever we went. She sometimes did not wait for people to ask her. She would say it before they asked.

The first day of school was horrible. I was excited to be in the same high school as my host sister. However, Heather was not that excited. I saw her during lunch and waved, but she quickly took her eyes off me. But, poor me, I followed her and joined the table with her friends. She introduced me and they seemed cool.

There was this guy she liked, so Heather kept staring at him the entire time. His name rang a bell. That was the guy she always talked to her friends about, on the phone and in person. I did not care much. I just wanted to belong.

After school, I went to the front of the school to wait for the bus, only to realize after a while that the buses leave from the back of the school. Drop off was in front of the school and pick up was at the back of the school.

It was weird. I had gone to a private school my whole life. This was a big school, over 1000 students with so many doors. After several trials, I finally got home with the help of a good Samaritan.

My host mom was so mad he'd brought me home. I explained to her that the school could not get a hold of her, so I told them my address and this guy said he lives not far away. I said my duas the entire time sitting at the back of his car with the window opened. I was remembering all the Taekwondo I had learned from GLISS. *If he tries anything stupid, I will kick him or hit his jaw and throw myself out through the window.* With my directions, he brought me home safely and I thanked him.

Now, my host family explained how the bus worked. I promised myself I would not miss the bus again.

The second day of school was better, but Heather seemed to be so absorbed with her friends and did not want me with them at the same table. Before I realized, she changed her lunch, so we did not have the same lunch break anymore.

The third day of lunch was sad. I sat on one of the long benches at lunch and everyone got up once I sat down. I felt off and sad. I quickly told myself, *"Sit by yourself. Don't let them feel that you are offended that they all got up."* I sat there and ate my lunch all by myself. All the other benches were filled either fully or partially, but I sat alone.

One day, our area coordinator, Ann, organized a picnic for all the exchange students in the same neighborhood, and I met Ami, Dion, and a Chinese student whose name I can't remember. He said he was attending BUHS, and I was so happy. I was like, "I am there too."

"We will have lunch together with our host siblings," he said.

I was dying to make friends. I met him in the hallway and waved at him. I was excited for lunch. *I will not be sitting alone*, I thought. I grabbed my lunch at lunchtime and looked for him and his siblings. I saw them and joined their table. He acted like he did not know me. I waved at him again, and he just nodded. He was cold. The entire time his host siblings ignored me, and I felt so hurt. I was just there but very invisible.

I felt like I was trying too hard. Well, I was. I just wanted to belong. I wanted to have friends like everyone else during lunch. I gave him the benefit of the doubt, but the same thing happened the following day. I advised myself to stop forcing myself on others. *I am good enough, and if they don't want me, that's fine. I will sit by myself.* And so, it was.

The following days and weeks were followed by me sitting by myself. Either I would sit somewhere and all the students at that table would get up and leave, or I would sit at an empty table, and no one would join me at that table. I started taking my books to lunch. As I ate, my eyes would be on my books so I could stop seeing all the filled-up tables and feel bad for myself.

Fortunately, I was acing my classes. But I was not happy. My host sister acted like she did not know me at school. She talked to me only at home. She was embarrassed to be with me outside. I was called names: *the Indian girl, the African girl, Hey!* And the list continues.

16

Trouble at Home in America

You would think with all the headache in school, home would be different. Well, the honeymoon stage was over, and the true colors of my host family came out now.

After dinner, it was TV time (news). They would always watch the same conservative news channel. The 2008 elections were coming up and I had no idea what was going on. They would smile when this man was shown and would be extremely happy. They spoke highly of him. I did not know him, but I liked him because my host family liked him. His name was John McCain, I later found out. He had an opponent whom they spoke bad of. I later realized it was a Black man. His name was Barack Obama.

Their face would fill with disgust when the Black man was shown on the screen. I was like, What did this man do to bring such pain to my family? They do not like him, so I did not like him too.

I went to school, and things were getting serious at school. The students had taken this election so seriously. They were campaigning, and it was funny to me. At the back of my mind, I thought, How can they vote? They are not 18.

Based on what I had seen and the constant ridicule and bashing of the Black man, I also believed he was not good. It was as though my host mom wanted to jump in joy whenever Mr. McCain spoke. However, whenever Obama spoke, she would get so irritated and chuckle.

My host dad was more collected and would look at me and ask, "What do you think?" I would just say, "I do not really know."

One day, I remember asking what the difference was between the candidates, and they said something outrageous about Obama, so I thought, Oh, then I do not want him to win.

At school, the kids would stop me and ask me all these weird questions. "How do you feel about wearing clothes now?" "Do you live with sharks in Africa?" "What food do you eat?"

I would get strange looks in the hallway because I decided to wear my African clothes more so they could stop asking me how it felt to start wearing clothes now. I always answered, "We have clothes in

Africa. This is from Africa." They also asked if Ghana was a village in Africa. To most of them, Africa was a country and Ghana was a city or village in it. It took some education and consistent repetition for them to understand that Ghana is a country and Africa is a continent.

Anyway, back to the election campaigns at school-things were getting heated. There were so many rallies during and after school. I would just shake my head in amusement at how serious and dedicated these students were in this election.

One day, one girl did not understand why I did not care about the election. She said, "This is historic. We are going to have the first Black president and you are not voting? You have to vote."

"Okay," I said. "Where do I vote?"

"We will be voting on Thursday next week," she said.

I said OKAY and left.

I came home happily, and during dinner, I shared how my day went. I told them about the school politics. My host mom quickly asked, "So who will you be voting for?"

I said, "Um, I don't know."

She got disappointed, and her whole face turned red. I was surprised she did not even know what to say.

Days afterwards, the school election was over, and a girl came up to me and said, "I hope you voted." There was a lot of noise in the hallways because people had voted and were sharing their votes with friends. She kicked me from behind and said, "Hey! I hope you voted, and I hope Obama wins." I did not care. Her friends came from behind and told me that Obama would win. They put a sticker at the back of my shirt and left.

I came home that day and my host mom asked me if I voted. I said, "No." She chuckled and kept looking at my back. I forgot there was a sticker on my back.

The whole evening was awkward. Everyone in the house kept giving me the looks. I did not know what was going on. I felt unwanted. Why am I feeling very uncomfortable?

I helped with dinner as usual. I set the table and we ate. After dinner, I did the dishes with Heather and headed to my bedroom. I read a few notes from the day's classes, and just when I was about to change for bed, that was when I realized the sticker at the back of my shirt that said, "I voted." I was like, Wow! This is what was making them mad, I think. They thought I voted and was lying to them.

Things just got heated, awkward and uncomfortable after that night. There was a lot of silence in the house in my presence. I did not feel welcomed. I had not felt welcomed in a while, due to the belittling of where I came from, the constant praise of America and American people over African people, the continuous pointing out of the poverty in Africa, and the list continues. Now, it was real. The heat was there, and you could tell. How do I explain myself? I thought. I thought time would tell, and they would forget.

School kept getting harder because I could not make friends outside of class. There was a new smart girl in my Geometry class whom I liked a lot. She sat with me, and we began bonding since she was new to the town and school as well. Just when I had settled in and became comfortable with her, she said she did not like it at school. She left the school after two weeks. I was heartbroken. The one friend I finally made had left. Brandy was her name.

Alhamdulillah, I was smart and always acing my classes, so it was hard to ignore me in class. That was when I enjoyed school. I answered most questions and complex problems as well. I enjoyed learning and the attention I got when I answered a question in class. People were forced to come to me for answers or ask me for help. Outside of class, however, they just passed me by like they did not know me.

It was strange for me because I thought we became friends since we had similar classes and I helped them in class. However, their definition of friends was different from what I was used to. In Africa, once you were in the same class and you talk a couple of times, you are friends; or at least you would wave or smile at each other in the hallways. It was different here.

Lunch was difficult to bear. The peak of the whole school lunch saga was one day when I ordered pizza for lunch. I asked for a slice of cheese pizza, and I was given bacon pizza. Hmm, the bacon was under the cheese. It was not visible like the pepperoni pizza.

I sat down at the lunch table and took a bite and realized I was chewing some meat, but I couldn't see any meat on the pizza. I took another bite and there was meat in my mouth again. This was when I tossed the pizza on the plate and walked straight up to the kitchen.

I faced the server fearlessly. "What kind of pizza is this?" I asked.

He said, "Cheese pizza."

I said, "No! It has some meat in it."

He said, "Oh! That is probably bacon." I remembered that bacon was pork.

I was like, "Wait! But I asked for cheese pizza, and I told you I don't eat pork."

He said, "Oh, I am sorry about that."

I tossed it in the garbage and ran out of the lunchroom area. It was like a scene in a movie. There was the kitchen, the lunch area, and then a small hallway where some teachers circulated the cafeteria for security reasons. I started running from the kitchen, all the way into the lunchroom area and then into the hallways.

The teachers were trying to stop me, but I did not budge. I went to the bathroom and tried vomiting. At the bathroom sink, I put my hands in my mouth, but nothing came out. I had drunk a lot of water before and after that pizza. I said, "Let me pee then." I forced myself to pee.

I came back to the sink and tried pushing my hands down my throat, but it did not work. Nothing was coming out. I started sweating. I remembered the story of Abu Bakr (may Allah be pleased with him) who threw up food that was given to him by money that was unlawful from one of his slaves.

I convinced myself that I could throw up. I went back to the lunch security men and asked them for the nurses' office. They asked me if I was okay. I said, "No, I'm not. I need to see the nurse."

The lunch break bell went off, signaling that lunch time was over. I did not care about going back to class. I just wanted to be like Abu Bakr and throw up all the haram (unlawful) I had just eaten even if it meant spitting blood. I ran to the nurses' office. I was breathless.

The nurse tapped my shoulders and asked me to sit and tell her what happened because she did not understand me. Mind you, I had an accent, plus I was speaking fast. I told her what happened, and she was asking if I had a pass from my class. I said, "I did not go to class after lunch. I just came here after trying to throw up several times in the bathroom."

She said, "Let me call your teacher and let them know that you are here." Time was ticking for me.

She did and came back to me and said, "Well, there is not much I can do."

I said, "Give me something that would make me throw up. I need to clean my system. I need to get the pork out of my body. It is forbidden to eat pork in my religion."

I was so hard on myself. She was confused. She just said she can give me something to aid me to use the bathroom and hopefully it would come out. That was not enough for me. I started shouting and crying, "I need to vomit and let this pork come out!"

I got up from the bed I was lying on and started throwing myself on the floor wallowing in pain and disappointment. I was forcing my hands down my throat and the nurse scolded me. "You cannot do this here," she said. "Young woman, this is dangerous, you can hurt yourself."

I started shouting and said, "I do not like it here! They lied to me at lunch. The guy told me it was cheese pizza, but it had bacon. Why? Why? Why? How do I get this pork out?"

I told her I did not want to go back to class, so I stayed there. She said she needed to monitor me, so I do not do something harmful to myself.

I did not understand Allah's mercy then. I thought Allah was mad at me, and He would not forgive me. SubhanaAllah! It was such a rough day. After several tries to throw up, only some spit came out, no pizza, no bacon.

The nurse took me to my last class since I could not spend my entire afternoon in the nurse's station. I thanked her but told myself that would be the last time I ate lunch at the cafeteria, and so it was. From that day, I arranged with my recess advisors and ate lunch in the recess room. If it was not possible, I ate in the hallway.

School was fun because I was learning a lot, and I loved learning new things. However, reality would hit me whenever I'd sit in the bus in the morning and after school and no one would sit next to me; and whenever it was time to go to the next class and I walked alone in the hallways. That is when I realized, I am not okay. I am different. I am black. I am a hijabi, modest and shy.

17

THE FIRST BLACK US PRESIDENT

After a series of heightened debates on TV and shouting and insulting the Black man, Obama, in the house, it was election morning. In my head, he was "the Black man," as his name hardly stuck.

My host mom got up early and left for work. That night from work, it was tense in the house. They had been discussing the election the whole time. I kept quiet because I could see how red her eyes were and how passionate her kids spoke about their experiences at school. Most kids were excited that day that America would be getting the first Black President. Others were not.

After dinner, they sat to watch the news righteously. It was as though my host mom wanted to enter the TV. I went upstairs. I was not interested. Any discussion of the election was met with a lot of heat, bad mouthing the Black man, and a lot of throwing tantrums, so I was not ready to be a part of it. I finished my homework and prayed 'Ishaa and went to bed.

The next morning, I was getting ready to pray Fajr when I heard a lot of banging downstairs. I opened my door and realized it was my host mom. She was getting ready to leave for work. That was weird. She usually leaves at 6:00 a.m. It was 4:45 a.m. She looked angrily at me and then took her eyes off me. She was banging her bag against the wall as she walked down the stairs.

"I am leaving for work," she said. "I am not eating breakfast because this damn person has become our President. I am not eating in this house because this Black person has become our President."

My heart started pounding. I was like, *Oh God! The Black man won. Wow! This is not good.* I was scared.

She slammed the door behind her. Breakfast was cold. I got angry looks from everyone. The house was full of angry people. I instantly knew my life would not be the same after this.

In school, people were happy. People were jubilating. There was a lot of excitement in the air; others were disappointed. That was the first day I felt visible. People would smile at me and say, "How do you feel to have the first Black President?" I would just smile and walk away. I wished I could be as happy as they were.

I later saw my host sister in the hallway, and she angrily passed by me. Not a *Hi*, or a *Hello*. I dreaded going home that day. I wished there was another house I could go to that day.

My recess advisors realized I was not happy, and I was thinking a lot during lunch. They curiously asked, "Are you not excited that a Black person won?"

I said, "Not really!"

They looked at me shockingly and said, "Why?"

I said, "Well, my host family don't like him."

"Oh, wow!" they said. "Well, that is okay, but you can like him and be happy."

"I don't think so," I said. In my mind, we were a family, so if they didn't like him, I did not like him either. I so badly wanted to be a part of the family and feel belonging that I was ready to do whatever so they could see that I loved them.

Going back home that day was like going to the graveyard. I was scared. I was saying lots of *duas*. I recited my *Quls*. I got home with cold feet. I rushed to my room and stayed there. I only came out to make *wudhoo'* and then went back.

After a while, my host mom returned, banging her pocketbook (handbag) on the kitchen counter. She had such a terrible day. "How did he win?" she said, angrily.

There was a lot of screaming and heavy words used, and I did not want to be a part of it. I did not come downstairs.

Later I checked the time, and it was almost dinnertime, so I decided to come down and help quickly. I forgot what we ate because it was such a mean day.

When I came downstairs, I greeted my host mom, but she did not respond. I thought she didn't hear me, so I repeated myself while coming towards her. But she turned her eyes away from me.

Heather gave me the looks and Michael was just looking away. Dad arrived and he just said, "Hey!" The atmosphere was awkward.

I was about to set the table when I heard a snap from the other side of the kitchen. It was my host mom. She took the plates from my hands.

"This is your plate, and this is your cup," she said, pointing to a multi-colored plate and cup. "That cup you took is Heather's special cup." She slammed the kitchen cabinet in my face.

I was in shock. *Since when did I have a designated plate and a cup?* They all ate in the white plates, and I ate in the colored plate. I immediately missed my real mom. I knew this was going to be bad.

After dinner, dishes were tossed in the sink angrily. I wanted to make things better, so I quickly started doing the dishes. I cleaned them all, but nothing I did was good enough. I cleaned the napkins and kept the kitchen clean. There was no "Thank you" from my host mom, who was panting in the house like an angry dog.

From then on, every day was a nightmare.

My host mom would say things that hurt me. She would say I looked at Heather some type of way. "Why did you speak to Heather like that?" she'd say.

Her kids would avoid me and keep me out of conversations. My host mom and host dad would watch their conservative TV channel that bashed this Black man, Obama. There was constant criticism of him that fed into the hatred they had for him. The joy on the face of my host mom when Obama was insulted as she watched this news channel was despicable.

I would just go upstairs to my room. No one talked to me. It was minimum conversation in the house. I was gradually breaking down.

Already, I was not making friends in school, and with the instability at home, life seemed unbearable. We would go out to eat, and they would all sit at one side and isolate me. However, my host mom was quick to introduce me as her exchange student from Africa.

I was isolated almost everywhere we went. When we went shopping and I was walking with them, I was told to walk by myself and meet up at the cashier. It was as though they were embarrassed to be with me. It was hurtful. Every day was painful. I would cry myself to sleep.

I started counting the days I had left to go back to Ghana. I wanted to be on the next flight back home. I could only e-mail my dad. I did not want to tell him what was happening. I did not want them to worry. I told them everything was okay.

Ann, our local program coordinator, could sense things were not okay through my e-mails. My emails had become short, and I was someone that liked to express myself a lot.

Ann called my host family and was met with series of whining. She paid us a home visit and was not thrilled about the outcome. We already had communication problems because I would not fully look into my host mom's eyes when I spoke. I did this out of respect. Apparently, in the American culture, that means you are lying if you do not look straight into a person's eye when you speak. Now, every little thing I did was magnified. I started hating myself, hating Obama and questioning my identity.

I hated Obama a lot. I felt as though my relationship with my host family would have been better if he had not won. I was really trying hard to be liked. I would do the dishes even if my host siblings did not want to help. I would take out the garbage, and I would help offload the groceries every weekend. I did my own laundry. I was really trying hard to be a part of this family. I would help with dinner; clean potatoes, pick up apples, squash, and some other vegetables from the garden, etc. I did everything to be liked, only to be rejected openly after Obama won the election.

I did not want to hear that name, Obama. It brought a lot of pain to me. I could see how that name traumatized my host family. *Since they are my family and do not like him*, I'd think to myself, *I do not like him either.*

Every day was a struggle. There was always something for them to pick on. Either my host mom or host siblings would find something to say or do that would ruin my day. My host dad was not directly hurtful toward me, but he was not supportive either. I could tell his wife ran the house.

18

Feeling Lost in a Strange Land

I had kids laughing at me at school. There was a time I got kicked. I asked her why and she sarcastically said, "Oh, I like your shoes" as she smiled slyly. I would hear people laughing when I passed by. Now, I was very sensitive. Anything little triggered me because I had taken so much at this point. People would ask if I showered. People would ask what food I ate. People would ask if we ate lions and whales. In the beginning, the ignorance was funny, but it got sickening as time passed.

I started disliking myself. I did not like that I was black. I did not like the skin I was in. I thought things would have been better if I were a different skin color. I did not like my skin color.

Nothing was going as I expected. School was getting difficult. People were asking all sorts of weird questions. People asked if I had sharks as pets. Also, there were some people that asked how I felt about being in a nice house here. Some of them asked if it was nice getting to eat the kind of food they ate here, and all kinds of ignorant questions. Oh, some even asked if I needed a washcloth to take a shower. Somehow, their ignorance made them think we are dark because we do not shower properly.

At home, I was yelled at. I was told not to take anything that was Heather's. It became almost unbearable living there. Each morning my host mom would just say bye to her kids before going to work but never cared to even talk to me. She would give them a hug or a kiss and wish them a good day. I'd just be listening behind the door in my room, but I would get nothing while she just walked away. I got used to it after a while.

My host dad was trying to be nice. He could sense the tension in the house, so occasionally, he would ask during dinner how school was going. My host brother was in the middle of it all. He wanted to be nice, but then he'd stop halfway or just run away. I realized there was so much pressure coming from his end, so he ignored me a lot.

You know how it is when you are in a room, and people are talking and making you feel invisible? That's how I felt. I did not feel cared for at all. I finally realized after some months of this torture that leaving that house would be best. I started a discussion with my program coordinator.

Once, there was a bake sale at school and I brought some baked goods home. I was new to all of this, so Heather checked out some things that she thought our dad would like, and it amounted to $18. I didn't know how it worked, so I just pointed out the baked goods that my host dad would like and said, "Yeah, this is what I got." But I didn't pay the $18.

After about two weeks of not getting the money, the lady in charge started writing me emails about paying the money, and they were all mean emails. I was like, *What is this?* I wrote to her saying, "I don't know what you're talking about. I don't owe you any money." We kept going back-and-forth.

She started threatening me in the emails. "Give us our bake sale money," she'd say. "This is ridiculous. It's over three weeks and you haven't paid it. Be careful before I send people to come get you."

Now, I really got mad, so I started thinking hard.

There were a series of emails that kept coming all the time, so I came home and discussed it with my host family. But only Heather got it, because I said, "Oh, do you remember the day I came home with a bake sale, and you took something? Do you know about any $18?"

She responded, "Oh yeah, I did, and that was for dad."

I said, "Well, that lady wants her $18 because she keeps emailing me."

Heather responded with, "Well, you were supposed to remind Daddy and get the money."

I looked at her shockingly. "I don't even know how it works," I said.

Later, my host mom came from work and then Heather told her what happened. The next thing I heard was I was being called loudly from my room. Then I was yelled at while she pointed her index fingers at me.

"No one yells at Heather!" she said. "Nobody in this house! I am her mother. You dare not talk to her like that."

I was speechless with tears rolling down my cheeks, and I ran upstairs. Nobody even asked my side of the story. I did not matter. I was just an exchange student in their house.

Whenever we walked or went somewhere, they would just walk together and try to isolate themselves from me in a way that people would not think we were together. However, if people asked about me, my host mom was very quick to say, "Yes, that's our exchange student from Africa" so that people would know I was not related to them in any way, shape, or form.

The following weeks just got harder and harder, no friends, no nothing. People you talk to, and you would think are friends, they didn't think so and didn't see you as a friend. It would be like, we just spoke yesterday and that was it. You would talk to them, and they would just look at you and walk away, so that was very different for me.

Things got out of hand and every day became very unbearable, so I reached out to my program coordinator, Ann. She paid us a visit and went over any issues the host family might have with me, and my host mom couldn't say much. It was a lot of whining about not understanding my culture, things that she never spoke to me about.

I said, "Well, hopefully, things will get better, and we can work things out now."

Ann explained to her that me not looking in the eyes of an adult is a cultural thing to show respect. However, my host mom thought I was lying by not looking in her eyes whenever I spoke. She felt it was disrespectful.

After that meeting with Ann, my host dad had a meeting with my host mom, and I could hear them talking in their room because my room was adjacent to theirs with the bathroom between us. I could hear them speaking loudly from the bathroom, and my soul would be aching.

Afterwards, it was weird because there was a lot of acting and everybody was trying to be nice, but it didn't last because it was fake. Things got out of hand again a lot, and it reached the point where just seeing me made my host mom want to throw up. So, there were days I wished I could change my face or the color of my skin just to fit in. I didn't like to look at myself in the mirror anymore, and to be honest I hated myself so much.

I just kept praying a lot and that kept me going. I'd stay in my room for the most part. We barely had any communication going. I'd say good morning, good afternoon, or good night, and that was it. I came out to eat, do the dishes, and go to the bathroom. That was basically it. I was just like a roommate in the house. I was compared to a cow and other nasty comments were made at me.

My host dad walked to my room one night and said, "You know, I wish things would have been better with you and Amanda." Amanda was my host mom. "But it's not," he said. "It is sad that things have come to this. But it's you and then my wife, and it's a difficult place to be. But I will have to side with my wife."

I said, "I know that, and I understand. I know this is hard, but I thank you for everything."

Ann called and told me there's an arrangement for me to leave that host family soon. "Just hang in there," she said. "I'll come pick you up next weekend."

It was the best feeling ever. I was like, *Finally!* because I was really going through a lot. I was crying a lot. The only time I was happy was when I was in class. At school, I was not happy during break, I was not happy during a hallway pass, and I was not happy when school was over because I was coming home to a house filled with cold people. I was careful not to step on anybody's toes or to say the wrong thing to anyone, because apparently anything I'd say or do, even just having my host mom see my face, was a problem.

19

Leaving My Host Family

I started packing my stuff and putting them in a suitcase. I was putting everything together on Friday before I left for a bowling game with Ann and the other exchange students in my neighborhood. It was marvelous; we had a good time. Ann asked me how I felt about her coming to pick me up during the weekend. I said I was good.

"I'm okay." I always had a smile on regardless of what I was going through. "I've been through a lot, but I'm strong," I said.

"Good to hear," she said.

It was the morning of the day I was leaving. I made sure I put everything in my suitcase. My host dad came and nicely said goodbye, and Michael was right next to him. You could see tears in Michael's eyes, but he was trying to hold it back. He waved at me from behind his dad, and my host dad said, "I wish you well." Heather was with her mother in the kitchen.

I came downstairs to get something, and my host mom showed me the recipe book that I'd brought from home. It was my mom's old recipe book, so I took that. Then my host mom gave me back the gifts I'd bought for her, my host dad, and her kids when I came from Ghana.

I told her, "No! This is for you."

"No," she said. "But you're going to a new family, and you need something to give to them."

I looked at her straight in the eye and said, "Where I come from, we don't do that. It's a gift for you. Don't worry about how I'm going to be with the new family. I'll be fine. I'll have something for them, don't worry."

She was so shocked and embarrassed that she instantly held onto the kitchen counter to stop her from falling. The gifts I'd bought them were expensive. I'd given them an original *Kente* cloth, a lot of jewelry, and cultural artifacts. But it was all for them, and I was not taking it back.

I never felt that good in a while. I had this strength that I never knew I had. I was smiling because I knew things would get better. I just had to leave this house to have clarity again and find myself.

She was disappointed. You could tell from her face. Apparently, she thought I would welcome the idea to take back all the things I'd bought for them, because earlier that morning, she'd come upstairs and took the sweatshirts she'd given me. There were two sweatshirts, a green one and a black one. She took them all back.

Now it was time for me to drag my suitcase down. My host dad was helping me with one, and I was dragging the other one by myself. I had my backpack behind me, and she didn't want to touch it. Heather was just following her mother, watching me drag my suitcase with much difficulty down the stairs.

Unfortunately, my host mom's mug was on the stairs. I didn't see it until my suitcase hit it, and Oh my God, it was like hell broke loose. She started cursing and yelling at me. I was like, "I am sorry. I didn't see it." I rushed to pick it up, but Heather pushed me and took it back upstairs.

"You're leaving the house," my host mom said, "so you must be careful before you leave."

I was like, *Oh, poor me, even this day was not drama free.*

My host family drove me to meet up with my program coordinator, Ann. We stopped somewhere, and I was told this was where we were going to part ways. I said thank you and goodbye to them. Michael just waved, but there was nothing from my host mom. I extended my hand to give her a handshake, but she refused. So, I thanked them for everything and just waved. I hopped into Ann's car, and that was the beginning of another experience.

I stayed with Ann for some weeks as she looked for a new host family for me. Ann was our program coordinator but was elderly and lived with her husband, so there was not much we could do together. Plus, the program had not expected her to host any of us. She only did this because my situation had become unbearable, and the headquarters asked her to get me out of there.

Interestingly, an African American diplomat was in town, and she heard about me. She decided to host me. I was so excited. I met her, and she had such a big smile. I was happy. She seemed nice. After showing me my room, I saw that she had idols, statues, and weird pictures all over her house. Naima told me that she hardly stayed at home. She moves around a lot because her children were spread out across the United States.

Naima shared some of her struggles with me, as an African American, working in a predominantly white neighborhood. It was nice to hear and see someone who understood my perspective. Our first day together was nice and peaceful. She lived by herself. We talked and laughed a lot. When it was time for prayer, she observed me pray. After prayers, she asked me a lot of questions about my faith.

Naima told me that she fasted in Ramadan. However, she combined all the religions. She believed in Christianity and Islam. She also practices some Buddhist rituals. She showed me the different

Buddhist monks and what they do. She told me they were powerful, and they protected her. It did not make sense to me. I remember *Sai Baba* well. She said he was God incarnate. I thought, "why will God come down in human form to save humanity?"

The next morning was peaceful. I woke up happy and peaceful, for the first time in a long time. When it was time for breakfast, she gave me a tea bag that had some horoscope readings on it. She said it will inform me about my day. I read it and smiled. That was interesting. "How can my fate be in a tea bag?", I thought. I walked to school since Naima lived close by.

After school, I walked back home, and it was beautiful. People rolled down their car windows and asked curiously if I was lost. Some people wondered if I was a refugee who needed help. I explained that I was an exchange student.

I came home to a calm house. I prayed, and Naima sat there saying her prayers to one of the idols. She had incense and candles all around her. After we both said our prayers, we met in the living room. She asked me why I was dedicated to Islam. Why do you pray? Your parents are not here. I said, "I do not pray because of my parents." I pray 5 times a day to God, not to my parents. She then said, "what if you find out that all that you believed was false?" I said, it is the truth. She said, how do you know? Because God says so in the Qur'an, I answered. Then she said, well, that is why I practice all the 3 religions so that whichever one is true, I am in it, and I do not miss out on judgment day.

It sounded convincing at the surface but foolish when you analyzed it. I told her that all the other religions lead you to God through someone, but Islam leads you to God directly. She said, "interesting". At dinner, she said I should stop eating beef.

"Beef is not good for you. Raw meat is not good for you," she said. I said, OKAY. I started reading about Buddhism and she gave me some leaflets. I was not convinced. It had some beautiful sayings about selflessness, but the reincarnation part did not make sense to me. God is One and All-Powerful. "If God wants to guide humanity, He should not have to come in the form of a human. That was the mission of the prophets He sent," I thought.

Our discussions were always civil and well-received from both sides. We were both very convinced in our beliefs but still respectful enough to listen to the other side. I loved that. The house was spiritual. I will recite Qur'an and say my prayers, and she will meditate, read the bible, pray to Buddha, and read some Qur'an too. My joyful memories with her were short-lived. Naima was called on duty, and she had to travel immediately. I had to move again. I stayed with Ann afterwards until she found me a new host family.

Alhamdulillah, I finally got a new host family, and they were amazing. The day I was moving to their house, I was nervous. I didn't know what to expect. Elizabeth, my host mom, whom I proudly call

Mom, was so amazing. They were funny and welcoming. It was awkward because I wasn't used to people being nice, you know.

Also, they liked Obama. There was on Obama sticker on their fridge. That freaked me out at first. In my head, I was like, *Is this a set up?* Ann was like, "Look, that is Obama."

They showed genuine interest in him, but I was skeptical of them because the first thing after welcoming me to the house was showing me a picture of Obama on the refrigerator. So, I was like, *Oh no! this is a set up because I had a bad experience. Now, they are putting me into a family that is acting like they like Obama.* I was skeptical about that. I wasn't as excited as they expected me to be.

This family was amazing though. Because of my last experience, I was not ready to try too hard to be liked anymore. I was me. They took me in as one of their own. My host mom always called me her African daughter. My host sister Mary Clare was amazing and loving. This family felt like home, but the trauma from the first family was so bad that I still couldn't accept something good. In as much as they were good to me, I had my guard up. *If they're faking it, it's going to end sooner than later*, I thought to myself. *The joy is going to end, and their niceness might not be true.* So, I did not expect much.

I really had a good time with this family. We would go out for dinner, and I was part of the family. They would walk side-by-side with me, and it was awkward for me. There would be times when I'd be walking fast or trying to isolate myself because I was used to that from the other family, but my host mom would be like, "Hey! Let's walk together."

She always introduced me as her "African daughter" or she'd say, "This is my daughter from Africa." It felt so good to not be referred to as an exchange student and to be part of the family. I was accepted. It was so hard to believe, so I would laugh and have a good time. But I would have doubts at the back of my mind afterwards. *Maybe, just maybe, they are faking it.*

20

Identity Crisis

I was going through a deep identity crisis. I was trying to find out who I was. What can I do to be liked? Maybe there is something wrong with me, and that is why the first family didn't work out. I was still questioning myself. What did I do wrong? What could I have changed to have made that work? How did it end the way it ended? I would see Heather at school, and she would give me this stern look and just walk away. I'd just shake my head and walk away.

Now, I finally had a friend. She was from Germany, and her name was Anna. She also had a similar experience with not enjoying her stay, but luckily for her, her program was only a semester long; so, she left to go back to Germany. She didn't have a good time either. Our friendship was short-lived, but we were able to console each other. It was nice. It was sad to know that we had been in the same school and didn't know about it until later, and just when we knew about it, time flew by quickly. I was grieving inside.

There was a concert at school that I attended with my host sister, Mary Clare. She quickly went in when she saw her friends, and I was left at the entrance with my ticket. The guy collecting the ticket said, "Hi. My name is Hunter, and can you please buy some cookies? We are having a bake sale. It is just a dollar."

I said, "Okay, give me two."

He said, "Thank you." I paid and left.

After the concert, somehow, he found me as I was looking for my host sister and wrote his number on a paper and gave it to me. He said I should call him and hang out. I said goodbye. He kept smiling at me. I smiled bashfully and left.

Do you know any person going through an identity crisis? You just fall onto that person that likes you or gives you attention. Hunter was that person for me. He seemed nice. I told my host mom about him.

At home, I'd just stay indoors on the weekends. My host mom kept asking me to make friends or try to hang out with some people. She asked me if anyone asked to be my friend at school. That was when I told her about Hunter, and that he gave me his number and said I should call him to hang out. She gave me the home phone and asked me to call him. I hesitated.

The following week, I think he met me again in the hallway and said hi. It was weird because he said hi from an arm's length and he didn't stop there but opened his arms and was going to give me a hug. I was thinking of how to tell him I don't hug boys, but I couldn't say it because he was right there in front of me now. I put both of my arms on my chest in a cross shape and closed my eyes and shouted, "No!" He just kind of froze and left me. After that he'd see me in the hallway and wave hi and I'd wave back, and that was it.

SubhanaAllah, making friends was difficult. I looked different. I'd come to class on a Monday and my classmates would be talking about how their weekend was exciting and interesting, and I just sat there quiet. My weekends were boring. They were spent just doing homework, grocery shopping, staying indoors, doing laundry, studying, and going on Facebook. That was all.

My host sister had a lot to do with her friends, so she was hardly home. My host mom asked me one weekend, what I wanted to do. I responded, back home, I always attended the madrasah (Islamic school).

My host mom was shocked, "Every weekend?" she asked.

I said, "Yes, for the most part, except when it was Eid, or we had a family visit or outing."

My host mom was really trying to get me busy and happy, but it was hard for me to fully give myself and hang out with her without having my guard up. I feared trusting her because of all the baggage from the old host family. I had a hard time navigating that, and I kept all this in.

After several weeks of this going on, my host mom was getting worried about me. She suggested I hang out with someone at least. She reminded me to call Hunter.

I said, "You know what? Let me call this person and see what he has to say. Maybe he can help me make friends."

I took the home phone and called Hunter. I said, "Hi, it is me, Mariam. You gave me your number. I am just calling to say hi."

He said, "Oh yeah! You want to hang out? I got a bike. Do you know how to ride a bike?"

I replied, "No! I haven't ridden a bike before."

"Do you want me to teach you? I could come pick you up and go teach you."

I'm thinking, *A guy going to sit on the bike and teach me how to ride it? Like, how is that possible? Is he going to go sit on one and then put me on another one, or are we going to sit on the same bike? That doesn't sound okay to me.* It was off.

I said, "Well, I'll think about it and ask my host family and then I'm going to let you know." That was it. I never called him back again.

So, he saw me at school, and said, "Oh, you never got back to me. I told my friends you were going to call me and then we were going to hang out."

I said, "Well, I just didn't want to go anymore."

As we were standing, a girl comes out of nowhere and gives him a hug and starts kissing him. That was weird, so I just looked down and froze. Then I looked to the other side and walked away.

This girl sees me the following day in the hallway and gives me the look. I was like, *Oh boy! What did he say to her about me?* I don't know, but apparently, she was waiting for him to come out of a class. Then I saw him coming out, and she ran quickly to him with open arms to hug him, but he saw me first because I was standing opposite his class. He started running across the hallway and unknowingly pushed her to the side, amid the crowd, and was coming towards me.

I was like, *I am not going to welcome this drama.* I waved at him and sped up my steps. But he caught up with me from the back and shouted, "Hey, why are you doing that?"

I said, "Why am I doing what?"

He said, "I was trying to say hi and you are ignoring me."

I said, "Oh well, I must get to my class."

He then said, "Oh okay! I thought you wanted to be friends."

That hit me hard. I was thinking, *This is my chance right here. This is the first person that really wants to be friends with me. I have always wanted to have friends at school, and I am always the one pushing myself on them. This is the first person that is pushing himself on me, and I just let him down.* That was the biggest test for me.

It hit me so hard. I was thinking about it for days. An inner voice was saying, *No, don't be friends.* But my heart was like, *This is your chance to belong and be like everyone else. This is your chance to have just one friend.*

I was thinking about it a lot, so I changed the route to my classes just to avoid seeing him, but I was always second-guessing myself. I told myself, *You're going to regret this. This person seems to have friends with him, and he seems nice. I can make more friends by becoming his friend.*

Why am I not open to being friends with him? I asked myself. *I can be friends with him, and he could teach me how to ride a bike. He can connect me with his friends in the school and just make me feel okay. But it seems like I'm pushing him away. Plus, he was so handsome.*

Something was off, it just didn't feel right. *This is not me, or something just isn't right about this friendship.* You know, my heart really wanted to be friends with him, but I couldn't do it. I couldn't bring myself to do it. I was slowly getting used to not seeing him in the hallway and having him ask about how my classes were going. I felt that cutting him off was the right thing to do.

One time, I was on my way to the library and guess what? Here he comes again with his smile, saying hi to me as I was approaching the library. He said, "You have no idea. I had a bad day and I need a hug."

I'm like, *Oh no! Not again! I cannot hug a boy.* I ran quickly to open the library door just to avoid him, and then he comes running and hugs me from behind.

I froze, blocking his hands from the sides. He was trying hard, and I was using my backpack (school bag) to block him. I did not want to try to get out quickly and he ends up grabbing me or hugging me more.

I looked up and said, "Yaa Allah! Help me!"

In that moment, his girlfriend sees us and stands there staring angrily at me. *Wallahi!* The story of Prophet Yusuf (Joseph), peace be upon him, came to my mind.

Hunter's girlfriend pulled him and took him to the side and started kissing him while staring at me.

I looked confused, took a deep breath, and walked away.

I was so mad at myself for not kicking him or stopping him from touching me. I had a lot of mixed emotions. Since then, I said to myself, *You know what? I must stand up for myself. This cannot continue. Maybe she thinks there is something between us.* I told myself, *It is not going to happen again. I am going to put an end to it.*

Now, as I walked in the hallways, I was on the lookout from all corners, ready to use all the Taekwondo defense skills I'd learned from

Junior Secondary School (JSS). I saw Hunter and gave him the cold shoulder, looked angrily at him, and walked away. I saw him in the subsequent days after that encounter, and I walked away briskly, seriously, and took my eyes off him. I snubbed him to be honest. He figured it out and left me alone. That was the end.

21

Finding My Way

I found comfort in coming on Facebook and chatting with my friends from back home who were in different states now. They seemed to be having a good time with their host families. There was no sign of Islam on most of the Muslims. They had made so many friends and seemed happy in their pictures. I knew I was in a good family now, but there was still always that doubt that something might go wrong.

My host mom loved me, but, just like every family, we had some misunderstandings here and there, which we talked about and cleared the air quickly. We would sit together and have conversations. They always said I sounded older than my age. I was only sixteen.

Any time I spoke with people, they said I sounded so mature. I thought that was a bad thing. I would quickly defend myself by saying, "I am just sixteen." They would say, "You sound eighteen or nineteen. You seem to have a lot of wisdom and know what you want in life. You are all grown up, girl." I would feel frustrated.

I took French class now, and I learned how to say beautiful things in French about my family. Miss Cassidy, my French teacher, really loved me. I'd talk to my classmates in French class because everyone wanted to be in my group. I topped all the tests and quizzes. To be honest, it was beautiful, and things were starting to fall in place.

The competition was getting tighter with me and a few people at the top. The school year was about to end, so I used any free time I had to study. That kept me busy.

I was getting comfortable in school now, and I started opening up to the female friends of my host sister. I'd ride home after school with Mary Clare sometimes. Other times, I'd take the bus, which took me to my host mother's school because she was a librarian there. I would then hang out until she closed. We would all walk to the house together.

My host mother was fit and beautiful. I sometimes got tired during the walks and occasionally complained because it was a long walk. Plus, the short path involved climbing a lot of mountains. Just like every mom, she would laugh about it and tell me to keep some of my heavy books at school in my locker, but I always wanted to have them to study. Let's just say this family was a breath of fresh air after what I'd experienced before.

We organized an end-of-year get together. I gave a speech which made them teary. I remember saying they did not only give me a bed to sleep in and food to eat, but they were there for me like a family, and I meant that. They were there for me. It was hard to leave because they were really kind.

Wait! Did I tell you about the school event with Mr. Montie (not his real name), the racist biology teacher? Okay. So, Heather my former host sister always spoke good about this man, and how he's nice and all that. I took his class and then I realized that he was racist. He hated me from day one. He gave me the looks and asked me if I was sure I wanted to take this class. I thought, m*aybe another Islamophobe.* He would pass over me and never assist me when I asked for help.

When we were learning something, he would ask, "Who caused this problem?" Then he'd say, "The Africans." He would answer and give me this disgusting look.

Once we were doing an experiment and a cotton ball was used. He burnt it and asked what happened to the color. He was like, "Let Mariam answer."

I said, "It turned black."

He shouted, "Black! Yes, black, just like you, just like the board!" Then he pointed at the blackboard. He added, "Just like her face!!!"

Another incident was the famous African bee story where he showed us a bee from our biology book. "It's called the African bee," he said. "All the problems are caused by these Africans." He gave me a devilish look.

Then there was a picture of a boy that was hungry and had "Kwashiorkor," which was a sickness that children who lack protein had. Mr. Montie made it sound really bad. He started giving all these false stories about how kids in Africa are always starving. "Oh, Mariam can tell us more," he said. "I bet she is happy that she is here with all the food she gets to eat here," he added sarcastically.

I wasn't laughing. I wasn't having it this time around. There was an Asian girl in the class who sympathized with me. She looked at me sorrowfully.

He made it look like that was how kids in Africa were, and he was asking me, "Oh, do you eat eggs, or is it something you get on special occasions?"

In my head, I was thinking, *Look at me. Do I look like that picture? So, why would you think everybody there is like the kid in the picture?*

He would put me on the spot. He would not miss a chance to make me feel bad; that was the epitome of his foolishness. He did not even know Africa was a continent and not a country. Well, maybe he did and was playing a fool.

After that African bee story and making everybody laugh at me for being black, I left the class and never came back. That was the last time I sat in his class. I went to my guidance counselor and dropped the class. He never gave me an apology even though my counselor said he would make him apologize to me. Apparently, he gave an apology to my advisor to convey to me.

Now, I realized why Heather liked him. Birds of a feather flock together; a racist befriends a racist.

My exchange year came to an end with an amazing graduation. I was a member of the National Technical Honor Society, which included the top 2% outstanding students in the school. I was fortunate. I also became a member of the Future Business Leaders of America (FBLA). I also got a Merit certificate in French class and a bracelet with the engraving *Mathematics* on it from my math teacher.

The exchange year was coming to an end. I shopped here and there. I was supposed to reply to colleges, but I did not, even though I got accepted to some. I was just excited to go back home and be normal again because of all that happened. My experience as an exchange student was not normal to me, so I lost interest in America. I ended my exchange year well, but there was always that doubt and hesitation about staying in the United States.

There was always that doubt in my mind telling me something might go wrong. *My host family can turn their backs on me any minute*, I told myself. You know, I would just take a walk outside, and there was the constant pressure of people looking out the window and asking me questions."Do you need help?" "Did you get lost?" "Are you a refugee?" "Are you okay?"

People would hold on tight to their kids when they saw me in the shops, etc. Others did not want to get their kids to walk next to me. Some feared me. Some people ran away from me. It was just a lot to take in. So, I just closed my mind on America. I said to myself, *You know what? I'm not going to come back here again.* That was it for me.

22

LEAVING AMERICA

Alhamdulillah, my host family was amazing. My host dad saw me off at the airport, and it was just so beautiful. His eyes were teary. I said goodbye to him. He didn't go; he made sure he stood there and followed me all the way down to the security. You could see him shaking his head and feeling sorry for me. Everybody else was just walking and going, and at this point, you know, I got used to this treatment. You know what it is called? Yeah, I think the artist Loon once said, "It's the Muslim special treatment." I was used to it at this point, so I didn't take it hard like I did in the beginning of the experience.

I finished. I was done with all the special searches. I waved at my host dad, and it was beautiful. He walked away, and I walked to the boarding room area.

I was sitting in the boarding area and just crying, crying so hard. I reminisced on everything that had happened. I was very teary and emotional. I was going to miss this amazing, incredible second family. I was imagining how horrible it would have been if I had stayed with the first family. I think I would have lost who I was completely if I stayed with them. I had an amazing second family, but the trauma from the first family still affected me until this moment.

Alhamdulillah! I boarded the plane to Washington D.C. to meet up with everybody. It was quite a sight to behold. We were all screaming. We had not seen each other in a long while. We were shouting and hugging. Everybody had changed. I was still in my hijab; a lot of people looked different. Some people had gone through an extreme change, others had a thicker accent than others. A lot of people had taken the hijab off from the Kenya group. I realized most of our Saudi students had become something else entirely. It was sad. You could not recognize most of them.

That was when it dawned on me. *Wow, is this what this experience was all about? We coming to America and changing who we are? Becoming this?* That was when it hit me hard. *What's the point of coming here and losing your religion?* I always had a smile throughout the hardship and everything that I went through. This orientation was a very interesting one.

I don't think we really paid attention to what was being said. We were more interested in catching up with each other and looking forward to the future. I could see my friends were so excited. Some people were coming back to the United States. I had college admissions in my mind. I had rolled up the college acceptance letters and put them in my suitcase. I was thinking, *You have no idea that I'm not coming back.*

It was a long flight back home, which gave me time to reflect. We missed our connecting flight and had transit in Europe, Amsterdam. *Alhamdulillah*, I got the chance to meet my father's friend there. We were on the same airplane to Ghana. It was beautiful. I didn't sleep the entire time on the flight.

When I got to Ghana, I was knocked out. I had not slept for two days. We had spent over five hours in Amsterdam. My parents were freaking out because I think I slept through the time for Fajr prayer, and I didn't wake up for Fajr until *Duha* time. This happened for two days in a row upon my return.

So, I remember my mom saying, "This is how you were living in America?" *I missed Fajr and they're making it a big deal,* I thought. That was the first time I missed Fajr in a long time. They did not understand that I was knocked out. I had not slept on the plane.

People were visiting me, and I was just happy to be home, giving gifts, and just seeing everybody. I was drinking the common water, *pure water*, as we call it in Ghana. People would visit and ask me, "Why did you come back? Who goes to America and comes back?" You know, that right there killed me. Because I knew what I saw. I knew what I experienced, and I should be back home feeling like, *This is where I belong, being so excited that I am not going back*. But the people that I thought loved me felt disappointed in me that I came back.

SubhanaAllah! That pain was worse than the pain I'd felt before. I felt lost, like I did not belong. I thought, *America did not want me, and then now Ghana, my home for the past sixteen years, doesn't want me either. So, who wants me? Am I Ghanaian or American?* During this silent crisis, I wanted to leave the house. I wanted to run away from everyone. Any program out there that was educational, I would attend. I wanted to leave the house.

My own parents were picking on me for the littlest things. When I'd speak, and I'd say, "Whatchamacallit" or "Oh crap," and everything I said was a problem.

Oh, I remember my dad was in the shower one morning. I had to pass a bar of soap to him, and I used my left hand and passed it to him. That was a big mistake. He talked down at me, screamed and complained to my mom.

Everybody was just picking on me, how I spoke, how I acted, how I sat, when I waved to people with the left hand, just little things. I didn't think it was a big deal. I'd just come back from a culture where I'd done these things for over a year, and it was not a problem. And now, suddenly, it was a problem. I would cry at night and question myself, *Was it worth it?*

I'd thought I was where I needed to be, but now it seemed as though where I'd left was better. I was now questioning my life in Ghana. There was this constant internal conflict. I really wanted to enjoy life in Ghana, but at the same time, there was the constant pressure from almost everybody back home telling me to go back to America.

I went to my high school to say hello to my teachers. There too, I had more of them questioning me. "What are you going to do now?" and "Why did you come back? What are you going to do here?" I'm like, *Why is everybody acting like this is a good question?* The program was made for you to come back, and then if you want to go back, that is on you. But I did not want to go back because of all the experiences.

I just kept myself busy. I always had something to do. I was at the AFS office on Monday through Friday, and Saturday and Sunday, I was at the madrasah.

I reconnected with some old friends. That helped me a lot. However, I didn't know how to deal with what I was going through inside. I had a lot of mixed emotions. I started not liking a lot of people because of how they constantly questioned my choice of coming back home. I got to a point of looking back at my experience and thinking, *Wow, I think I would have been better off there instead of having people that I love telling me that I'm not wanted.*

Gradually, I went through a phase of accepting all the noise and what happened. I started to think, *Maybe I'm the problem. Maybe I'm not good enough. Maybe I should have stayed. Maybe people don't want me here because they moved on without me.* I caught up with my high school friend, Hawa, and we went through the search for university together. Later, my cousin Hairrat joined in as well.

PART THREE

MEETING MY HUSBAND

"Patience does not mean to passively endure. It means to be farsighted enough to trust the end result of a process. What does patience mean? It means to look at the thorn and see the rose, to look at the night and see the dawn. Impatience means to be so shortsighted as to not be able to see the outcome. The lovers of God never run out of patience, for they know that time is needed for the crescent moon to become full."

—Elif Shafak, *The Forty Rules of Love*

23

Starting University

I thought of attending Ashesi University, which is like the American university in Ghana. It was expensive and the fees were excruciating, so I ended up going to Valley View University with Hawa, my high school friend, and my cousin Hairrat. We were like the three musketeers, fully clothed in hijab, and it was a shock to a lot of people because they thought we were from Nigeria.

Valley View University is Ghana's Premier Private University. It has a lot of rich kids from all over the world, with a large population from Nigeria. There were a few people from America and Britain as well, and we had students from various African countries. It was expensive to attend, but not as expensive as Ashesi University.

My experience in the early days was not without drama. There was this lecturer (whom I will call Mr. Nosy) whom I never liked because of this experience I am about to share with you. He saw me, Hawa and Hairrat and you know, he gave us this awful look. We came to the business office asking a question about some math entrance exam that we had to take that we hadn't seen earlier. He ignored us. We figured he might not have heard us.

He looked up at us and said, "Well, you know you must read here. This is a school. You have to pay attention. When you see things, you read, okay?" He was talking to us in a degrading manner. I got so upset and offended.

I did not like him since then. I never did for the entire four years, and I still don't like him. I don't think I'll ever like him. He continued to show hatred towards us for the entire time we were there except for Hairrat because she took a banking and finance course with him. But for me, no! I never took any class with him.

I chose my classes carefully and made sure I did not cross paths with this person. The only encounters we had with him were several instances where he would force us to go for worship. It was called the "Week of Spiritual Emphasis." He stopped us on campus and started shouting at us about the golden rule. He said, "You have to go to church!" However, the rule was for the students who lived on campus. We were off campus, but he said, "It doesn't matter." We ignored him and walked away.

I ultimately enjoyed school. Now, I was away from family and friends and in a whole different environment of people who did not know me. This was the perfect opportunity to challenge myself to be who I wanted to be.

I was now confident and fearless. The real me was coming out. All the things that I had gone through in America and my identity crisis back home were pushed aside. Now, I was at the University, where I could live and be myself without anyone telling me what to do, without the pain of whatever America did to me, without everybody being in my business. I was healing from whatever the past years had brought. I enjoyed it.

My confidence was apparent. I faced everyone and anyone. I was not scared at all. I was free spirited. I was blossoming. But the beautiful thing was that my dad always had my ego in check. I would come home for the weekend, and he would just throw advice at me here and there. He would say things like, "I don't think you are all that. Going to University does not mean that you are done."

This might sound harsh, but these were the things that I needed to hear because of the kind of person I was becoming. I think he could sense from the way I spoke and did certain things. I wanted to do things my way, and his remarks from time to time kept me in check.

My roommate was an amazing influence. May Allah reward her. You know, there would be times we would just be going on with our lives and she would say, "Let us take a pause and fast on Mondays and

Thursdays." We listened to lectures and reminders together. We prayed together. We saw with our eyes how everyone could do whatever they wanted. Our parents were not there, but we both knew that Allah is watching.

I cannot emphasize enough the importance of having a good Muslim roommate. *Wallahi*, simple things like sneezing and someone saying "*Yarhamuka-Allah*" (May Allah have mercy on you) or coming inside the room with "*Assalaamu Alaikum*" (Peace be upon you) and eating with the right hand and saying "*Bismillah*" (In the name of God) before eating. It has such a huge impact on a person's identity. We lived Islam and we were not shy about it. We had each other's back, *alhamdulillah.*

We were well-known because we were the only three girls in full hijab. I was mostly with my roommate, Hawa, since my cousin was coming from home to campus. She did not live too far away from school. We were smart in all our classes and enjoying school. We stood out in a good way and that felt good.

24

Meeting My Future Husband

My time at the university is intertwined with how I met my husband. Now I am going to be sharing with you my late teenage years together with my pre-marital life. So how did I meet my husband? This is one question that comes to mind when I think about marriage.

A lot of people have different made-up stories about it. Some said he came out of nowhere and took me away. Some people said I married him because of "America". Some people said I married him because we speak the same language. Others are still in shock after all these years about how we met and how we got married.

Let me tell you what happened. Sit back and enjoy.

It was 2010, a year after my exchange year abroad. I was busy with volunteerism at my Alma mater (GLISS), the AFS office and attending madrasah on the weekend. One day, my grandfather was sitting in the house chatting with a well-dressed man. He was in a suit, and they were having a laugh. I was called upon to bring some water for the man to drink and take a picture of them. I came and did just that.

This gentleman was in awe. You could see he kept looking at me but would quickly avert his eyes when I raised my head up after my grandfather finished talking to me. My grandfather was telling me who the gentleman was and what he did. All I got from the story was that he worked at a bank, and he was a good guy. I did not make a deal of it. I smiled to my grandfather and left.

A couple days later, I got a phone call, and it was the gentleman. Typical me, I was so straightforward. "Who are you, and why are you calling me?" This was what I said after responding to his salaams and hearing a man's voice. *SubhanaAllah!*

He calmly replied, "My name is Sabtiu, and I was the guy who was with your grandpa some days ago and you took a picture of us."

I said, "Oh ok." Then I asked, "So how did you get my number? What do you want?"

He was taken aback. He said, "I just wanted to say thank you."

"Okay," I said and hung up.

I approached my grandpa shortly afterwards to confirm the guy's story. He said, "Oh yes! I gave him permission to speak with you."

I was like, "Oh okay. I didn't know that. He called and I was so upset. I even asked him how he got my number."

My grandfather smiled and said, "He likes you." I pretended that I didn't hear and was about to leave his living room, and he repeated it louder this time. "He likes you. He is a good guy. He would make a good husband."

I ran out as fast as I could. I was in shock. *How can I just meet a person by serving them water and taking a picture and then they decide they want to marry me? Like how? He doesn't even know me,* I thought.

Since then, I started playing hide and seek with my grandfather. I would avoid him and run away from him whenever I saw him. When he was in the house, I stayed indoors and never came out to the compound.

The poor guy did not call again. I didn't hear from him again, so I thought that was it. My busy life moved on, attending programs, and emceeing them. There was hardly any Islamic seminar, convention, or talk that I would not attend.

One day my grandfather called me. I could not escape because he called me in front of my dad, so I quickly went. He said, "Have you heard from the guy again?"

I said, "No!"

He said, "Oh! Do you know he will be going to America soon?"

I was dancing inside. I was like, *Woo-hoo, that is it. He will go, and he will never see me again.*

My grandfather said, "I asked him to reach out to you for help since you just came back. He wanted to know what are some of the things to expect and what he should buy."

I was like, *Oh boy!*

Sabtiu came to our house again on a Friday. This time he was wearing African clothes. That was the tradition for the bankers. They wore their suits from Monday to Thursday and then Friday was a casual day. I knew this because I wanted to be a banker too, not because I loved it, but because my mom loved it and always had such respect for the ladies that attended to her at the banks. I wanted to be a banker to keep and protect my mother's money. Anyway, back to the banker's story.

I was eating when my dad called me to come and say salaam to someone. Mostly, my dad would not call us when we were eating. He would say, "Finish and come." But this time, he still asked me to come even though I was eating. That surprised me. I came out and guess who I saw? The gentleman, Sabtiu, again smiling with my dad and being all comfortable. I was shocked. I wanted to put him off.

My dad said, "He asked of you."

I said, "*Salaamun Alaykum.*" I started licking my fingers to put him off. That was not lady-like. Sabtiu just kept smiling. There was nothing to say.

My dad was smiling at me and smiling at him. It was awkward and quiet, so I said, "Let me go finish my food." I nodded and responded to his salaam and walked away.

Gradually, this gentleman was becoming friends with my dad. Now he had my grandfather and my dad on his team. My dad started telling my mom about him. I overhead them one time when we were watching TV. Dad said, "He knows his background and lineage. He is from a good home and a good family." I brushed it off and moved on with the show.

Not long after that, his date to leave for America was approaching. He had a week more. He contacted me again upon my grandpa's insistence and asked me where he could get some jackets and warm clothes to buy. I told him where he could get some of them. For the rest, I told him I would have to go with him because I could not tell the exact location on the phone. You know how we do not work with addresses much in Africa, right? It was a lot of corners and markets that you could not just tell someone. You had to go with the person to show them.

Sabtiu agreed. I figured this would be my first test for him. *Let me see how he handles himself.* I finished volunteering at the AFS office one afternoon and he asked me to come over to his workplace, Ecobank, so we could go together after work. I asked for permission, and my mom allowed it since it was in the afternoon, and it was in an open space. We tried getting my brother to join us, but he had something else to do.

I got to Sabtiu's workplace and asked of him. The security man showed me his office. Sabtiu was closing his register. He was in a flawless suit, very well dressed, *maashaaAllah*. I was impressed. *Such a well-dressed Muslim man*, I thought. He waved and said salaam. He offered me water and went back to finish off. He soon finished, and his colleagues were making fun of him. Apparently, this was the first time a lady had come looking for him.

Somehow, they all assumed I was his fiancée. I was receiving congratulations from all corners, and I started shaking my head. I was like, *What did I get myself into?* Sabtiu sensed I was uncomfortable, so he quickly told them I was his sister. They were teasing him more now. He led me out of there and called for a taxi.

He opened the door for me, and he went through the other door. I kept directing the driver to where we were going. This is normal for us Africans. We do not always have an address to where we are going. We figure it out as the driver drives sometimes. This was one of those cases. We finally got there, and I saw one of the stores and asked the driver to stop. Sabtiu paid him, and we left.

We bought some jackets, and Sabtiu was very well behaved. He asked me if it was okay to add me as a friend on Facebook since he was leaving soon, and he wanted to keep in touch. He insisted he did not want to bother me with phone calls, and Facebook would be easier to leave a message. "So, you can respond when you can," he said.

I thought that was wise. I said, "Okay." I gave him my Facebook name and he added me.

We took a cab back home and he made sure I got home safely. He walked me to the door and left. I was impressed. *Such a well-mannered guy*, I thought.

The following day, it was as though my grandfather was updated. He called me and asked how yesterday went. I said, "It was okay."

He asked, "What do you think about the guy?"

I smiled and ran out.

25

Separated by an Ocean

Now, his mom wanted to meet me. I was like, *You barely know me, and your mom wants to meet me?* Before coming, he asked about buying an American dictionary. I told him that it was not necessary, but he bought it anyway. I went to see his mom with my younger cousin. We met at his grandma's place which was not too far away from us. It was a ten-minute walk. I got there, and there was his grandma, mother, and sister. I almost went back when I saw everyone. *Alhamdulillah*, I went with my cousin because I was taken aback..

They warmly welcomed me, and he was sitting in the middle of all of them. He asked his final last-minute questions. Where should he put his money, tickets, and visa? What should be in his carry-on bag? and so on. I answered, and he thanked me.

We heard the *azan* for 'Ishaa, and he thanked me and left for the masjid. I thanked his family and left. I said, "We will pray at home *inshaaAllah*."

He left for America the following day and sent me a message on Facebook when he arrived. I said, "*Alhamdulillah*" and that was it.

We did not have any meaningful discussion for almost two years. Let me just say, I avoided him and did not respond to his messages. All this while, he kept speaking to my grandfather and father and was friends with my brother on Facebook as well. From time to time, I would hear about him when I came home for the weekend from university. He hardly posted anything on Facebook. He just had his profile picture of him, in a suit, of course.

He travelled to America, and I started university. It was such a busy time for me. I was busy with school politics, studies and fighting hard to establish a Muslim Students Association on campus. I came online one day, and he said, "Salaam." I responded and he asked of the family and how everyone was doing. He kindly asked me, "Did you see my email?"

I said, "No."

He was quiet for a long time. He said, "I sent you an email which contains a message that I cannot tell you in person."

I said, "I will check and get back to you."

The poor guy had sent the message not long after he had arrived in the USA. I realized how backdated it was and felt bad for him. He was basically expressing his interest in me and that he wanted to marry me. It was so touching and so respectful, yet so direct. What stood out for me was where he said, "I want you to be my wife" or "I see my dream wife in you." That was nice.

My dad had also told me about his interest, but I did not give my dad any response. However, my response to Sabtiu was, "No."

It was not because he was not good enough. It was because I did not want anything to do with America after my experience. I did not want someone who was there. However, Sabtiu did not give up.

After a while, Sabtiu reached out again to my dad. He spoke to his grandma to officially send a proposal to my dad on his behalf. She did and I remember I was washing clothes one Sunday morning when she arrived. I was sick to my stomach. I felt bad making his old grandmother come out that early on a Sunday morning. I welcomed her, and she asked of my dad. I said he was inside the living room. She went inside. I offered her some water and went back to washing the clothes.

I heard my dad saying, "Don't hold my legs please. You are my "Aunty" too. I will talk to her and get back to you, *inshaaAllah*."

She came out and looked at me and left. I felt uneasy because I heard "I will speak with her." I quickly planned and left back to campus that afternoon. I planned not to come home for a long time.

After two weeks, my mom said to me, "It has been a while since you came home for the weekend."

I said, "I've been busy with school stuff." At the back of my mind, I was avoiding the "marriage talk."

She said, "I would like you to come home next weekend."

I could not say no to my mom, so I came home that Friday evening. Everything was normal and no one said a word about it. In my head, I thought, *Dad took care of it. Well, he has always done so until now, why would he change?*

Several guys had come to ask for our hands in marriage and my dad had turned them away. He would only tell us after a long while and say, "They were not marriage material, so I did not bother asking you." My dad explained to us what a good man should possess. I loved my dad, so for me, I wanted to marry a man like him. I always said to myself, *If my dad says no, then I will say no. If he says yes, then I will say yes too.* In my head, I thought, *It means he told this guy no too.*

It was Saturday and everyone had gone to bed. We were watching wrestling, I think. Out of nowhere, my dad cleared his throat and started talking about the gentleman, Sabtiu. My dad said, "Sabtiu's grandmother came here to ask for your hand in marriage on his behalf. She said you should not worry or be scared. He wants to marry you."

I did not see this coming. My dad told me his background and told me stories about his father, may Allah have mercy on him, Ameen. I was shocked. The way my dad was talking about him was in the affirmative. *Did he already say yes to the guy?* I was nervous. I started sweating. It was as though I was sitting on hot coals.

My dad said, "What do you think?"

I was silent for about thirty minutes. I just looked down. My dad got tired of the silence, and my mom was just smiling and comforting me. Daddy said, "You should tell your mom, if anything."

I got up and went to bed. I could not sleep that night. *Marriage? Me? Was I ready? What will I be doing with someone who lives in America? Racism? Pain and suffering?*

I woke up the next morning with a headache. I went to my grandma. She was my source of comfort in complex situations. She consoled me. I was in distress. I started crying. She realized my worry. She explained, "Proposing and accepting does not mean you are getting married right away. You will have to know him first. It just means he has shown interest with the possibility of marriage."

I said, "But I don't know him."

She said, "He is a good guy. We know his background. Your dad has done detailed research on him. We know his parents' side, and he has good morals."

I said, "But people change in America. What if he has changed?"

She said, "Sabtiu spent several years in Qur'an school, and he is a person of the Qur'an, so there is no way he could change. If he would change, he would change for the better."

I was not fully convinced, but I did feel better. I quickly packed up and prepared to leave for school. Dad asked, "Why are you leaving so early?"

I said, "I have some homework to finish."

The ride from Nima to Madina was chaotic. I remember the mate (the guy who collects the fares on the bus) screaming at me, saying that we had arrived. My mind was heavy. My thoughts were flooded. I remembered all the racist things I'd gone through. *I do not want to go to America*, I thought. *I just want to visit my second host family, but I do not want to live there.*

26

Conflicted Inside

Since I did not say anything to my dad about Sabtiu and every time I was asked about him, I was quiet, my dad took this as my acceptance of the proposal. So, one day "Mr. Handsome" called happily thanking me for accepting. I was like, "What? I said no."

Sabtiu said, "Oh! But your dad called my grandma and gave his blessing."

I was like, "Well, maybe he said yes, but I say no."

Sabtiu was devastated. His whole family was in a celebratory mode, and I killed the poor guy's spirit.

Deep inside, I was conflicted. I had told Sabtiu earlier that I say what my dad says, but I was not living up to my words. Now, it seemed that I had not meant what I said. I am generally a person of my words, but not this time. I let myself down. It was hard for me to accept that my dad liked Sabtiu. I thought my dad would treat Sabtiu just like he did the other guys who'd come before him. I guess there was something special about him.

Sabtiu was patient. He persevered. "You will be my wife. I will marry you *inshaaAllah*," he said. "From the first day I saw you, I told your grandfather that I will marry you, and it would happen *inshaaAllah*." I laughed when he said that. He was a good guy, but I was so afraid to commit to something I was not sure of.

I started telling my mom my fears and she would console me by sharing stories of her and Daddy's engagement and marriage story. She would tell me stories about his mom and how loving she is. All this while, I was not addressing the real problem: *fear of racism*.

Sabtiu had a strong Islamic background. He was teaching kids at the madrasa every weekend in the United States and was schooling and working during the weekdays. He loved his grandmother to death, and he loved his mother and sister dearly as well. He was family oriented, and I liked that.

Everything about him was good, but I just did not want to live with him in America. My dad blessed us to get to know each other, saying, "Maybe you will feel better about him."

My mom expressed my concerns to my dad, and he would help clear them as much as he could. They answered all my fears and concerns, at least the ones I spoke out loud. However, I did not tell them what was really holding me back: the fact that he was in America.

27

Losing Grandma

My grandma, who is probably the person I listen to the most, gave her blessing. *SubhanaAllah!* Even on her last days on earth, she blessed me and blessed the union. I was so worried about her health that none of that mattered. I spoke with her, and we made dua together. She got better after seeing me that Friday. She and I spoke a lot. I made *ruqyah (spiritual healing prayer)* for her in her drinking water and she drank it. She later fell asleep.

After I put her to sleep, I came to our living room. I told my parents, "Grandma is sick, and moving forward, we should all say the *Shahada* when we visit her in her room so she can say it."

My cousin immediately interjected, "*Ehern!* You are back. Who said she is going to die?"

I said, "You do not have to be dying to say the Shahada. Let us just keep saying it with her."

Saturday morning, Grandma's condition worsened. She was not eating. She was in a lot of pain. I was her favorite grandchild because I listened to her a lot and took her advice. She shared so much wisdom with me. She shared family stories and history with me, so I know so much about our big extended family through her. She was still not eating.

"I am going to call Daddy, your son," I told her. She looked up.

I called my dad and asked him to come and tell her to eat. We mashed some kenkey for her with some milk and sugar in it. *Allahu Akbar!* Once she heard her son's voice, she raised her head up and opened her mouth. I put the cup on her lips, and she slowly sipped and sipped.

"She is eating now! *Alhamdulillah*!" I shouted.

She drank a sizeable amount and started shaking her head. I asked if she was full, and she nodded.

I said, "*Alhamdulillah.*" I cleaned her mouth, and she slept on my thighs. I was scared. Something was telling me Grandma would not make it. I was scared to voice it out loud. Already, I had been chastised for telling people to say the Shahada when they come to see her. I left her and took a shower and changed my clothes.

I came back and she said she wanted to sleep. She advised me and said, "Everything will be okay." She started speaking Hausa. We are Kotokolis and we speak Kotokoli at home. *Why is she speaking Hausa to me?* I was worried. She was saying things that were not making sense. She was making lots of duas and I was saying the Shahada for her.

She was nodding and when someone came to visit, she started asking, "Who is this?" She got worse in the evening, and she was rushed to the hospital.

Alhamdulillah, she was brought back on Sunday morning. I came to her, and she drank a little and slept. I was preparing to leave for school, but I did not want to. It was getting dark, and I had to leave. I spoke to her, and she smiled. She lay on her pillow and slept. Her head was hot. I made dua for her and kissed her on the forehead before I left.

A voice said to me, *This might be the last time you see her.* I came back again and remembered all the advice she had given me in these past days. "I will make you proud," I said. "Feel better." I kissed her again and left.

I called immediately I arrived at the hostel and was told she was okay. She had eaten and had gone back to sleep. *Alhamdulillah*, I was then able to eat something too. I drank some tea and went to sleep.

I had an early class on Monday, at 7:15 a.m. I called home after that class to speak with her. *Alhamdulillah*, my dad said she was okay and had visitors. *Alhamdulillah*, I was so excited. *She must be feeling well to be welcoming guests and talking to them*, I thought. *Alhamdulillah.*

Tuesday was a busy day and I forgot to call. When I was about to sleep, I remembered and called. Dad said she was okay and had gone to sleep already. I said, "*Alhamdulillah.*"

I had a sleepless night. I kept tossing here and there. Just when it was almost Fajr, the sleep started coming and before my alarm went off, a call came through. It was from my mom.

For the two years I had been at university, my mom never called me before Fajr. I sensed this was bad news. I picked up the call and she relayed the news, "Allah has taken your grandma back."

"*Innaa lillahi wa innaa ilaihi raajioon.*" *Indeed from Allah we came and unto Him we shall return.,* I said. *May Allah have mercy on her. Ameen.*

I fell on the bed. Shortly thereafter, my alarm for Fajr prayer went off, and my roommate opened her eyes to a teary me. She asked what happened, and I told her.

She consoled me after saying, "*Inna lillahi wa inna ilaihi raajioon.*" We made *wudhoo'* and prayed Fajr. I could not feel my feet. I fell on the bed after Fajr.

We had an early class that day. I told her to tell the teacher what happened to me and why I would be missing class today. She said, "Oh no! I am coming with you. I am not going to class either." I was relieved and shocked at the same time. She was sacrificing her class time to be with me.

We walked to the bus stop to board the *trotro* (public transportation) to the house. I was teary and speechless. The entire ride I was praying someone would call and say my grandma woke up from sleep. After a long hour and a half, we arrived at my house.

It was surreal. It was hard to walk to the house. We were walking towards my house, and I saw people sitting under tents crying. Some people began consoling me as I walked towards them. I was sad, but I was trying really hard to keep it together. All eyes were on me. My grandma and I were so close. She was my favorite grandma. She was my advisor. She was the one who believed in me like nobody else. My grandma believed I could do anything. If you dare her on anything about me, she will tell you I could do it. She was my biggest fan.

I walked to the gate of the house, and it took a lot for me to walk through the main door. I finally did and greeted my aunt, whose door was the first in the house. I greeted everyone else and walked to my grandmother's room. She was inside the bedroom. She was covered with a white cloth. I asked if they had given her a bath and they said, "No." I kissed my grandma, and tears rolled down my cheeks. I quickly left the room.

I now walked out to our room and greeted my mom. My dad was wondering how I heard about it. I think he did not want them to tell me just yet. I told Mommy I would help her with the bath. I wanted to make sure the right people gave my grandma the *ghusl* (ritual bath).

I changed and went back. I made dua for her. I made a lot of dua. People in the house were all looking at me anytime I came out. I got some water in the bucket and went back to the bedroom. My aunt got some sponges, and I got the perfume and scented stuff for the water.

We gave her the *ghusl*, and it was so emotional. As we were turning her body gently to the other side, I almost said, "Grandma fix your head." Her head was almost falling off the edge of the bench. I quickly went up to her head area and fixed it. *SubhanaAllah!* This makes me emotional just recalling. *Alhamdulillah*, everything was done, and we were called to see her for the last time.

It was so emotional seeing my dad. His eyes were red, and his voice was shaky. He was holding it together. My mom reminded me to take *ghusl* since I'd given grandma a bath. I did not know this then. *MaashaaAllah.*

Dad made sure everything was done properly, and my grandma was taken out on our busy street for the Janazah (Muslim funeral prayer). We finished the Janazah prayer, and her body was raised up, and that was when I lost it. I ran back to the house crying nonstop.

I cried a lot and did not eat. My mom encouraged me to eat a little, but my mouth could not chew or swallow anything. I was crying soberly and made sure my roommate was fed.

People were eating. Some were laughing and making jokes. I was looking at the whole atmosphere. People were moving on like nothing happened. It hit me so hard how short life is. *They have forgotten why we are gathered here already*, I thought.

When it was sunset, I left to go back to school. My life from then on was not the same. I could not function anymore. I lost interest in everything. I did not eat for three days, relying on only liquids.

28

School Life

I did not go for the award ceremony. I was the Overall Second Year Best Student for Management. My course mate, Judith Anagli, called me on the phone and asked, "Where are you?" I told her I was at the hostel. She said, "Your name was mentioned several times, but you were not there."

"It doesn't matter," I said. "I lost my grandma."

"I'm sorry," she said and hung up.

The next two months were the toughest. Everyone at home thought I was okay because I would come home for the weekend and act like I was okay because everyone expected me to be okay. But really, I was not okay. I struggled a lot. My grades faltered. *Life does not matter*, I'd be thinking. *In the end, you will just die.*

All this while, though my scores had faltered a bit in my assignments, I was doing amazingly well in school. I was fiercely fighting for the formation of Ghana Muslim Students Association (GMSA), VVU branch. I was on the Dean's List at the end of every semester. I was at every seminar and workshop with my roommate. She and I wanted to enrich ourselves.

However, after my grandmother passed away, nothing was important to me anymore. I remember writing on my Microeconomics final paper, "I lost my grandma, and nothing matters." I was not in a good place.

I had sleepless nights. Shaytaan (Satan) started playing with my mind. I could not be in the room alone at the hostel. I was always scared. I would be on edge whenever I washed my face in the bathroom. It was as if I would see my grandma in the mirror. I was seeing things and hearing voices.

Alhamdulillah! Sabtiu understood and gave me my space. It is not like Sabtiu checked on me often anyway.

It was now 2013, and this gentleman reached out to my family again with a proposal for marriage. This time, I told my mom I was not on board. She was sad. She said, "He is a good guy though. Your dad likes him." My mom knew how much I loved my dad. I just smiled and went back to school. I did not want to hear about Sabtiu anymore.

Sabtiu would call to speak with me when I came home for the weekend. He was so respectful. He called and asked of everyone and made sure he had a short and meaningful conversation. I respected him for that.

This continued for a while, but there was no progress. His family was getting restless. I remember his grandmother coming to see my dad again. She wanted a response. I said no, but my dad told her, "I'll let her come over."

I loved old people, and for me, this was a moment to reflect and reconnect with Sabtiu's grandmother like my own grandmother. I visited her for several hours sometimes when I came for the weekends. His family loved me, and he loved me. Unfortunately, the feeling was not mutual. I cared for his family and wished the best for him.

He never gave up. He would check on my parents and siblings. He was family oriented. He always said, "You will be my wife." I used to laugh, and in my head, I was like, *Yeah right!*

I was involved in *da'wah* (sharing Islam with others), and there were some *da'wah* guys that I kind of thought, *Yeah, he has some qualities that I like.* I would think, *He is right here in Ghana so that would be easy since I can see and tell who he is.* Then I'd think of Sabtiu. *This gentleman is in the U.S., and he might be different than he portrays himself.* That was always my fear.

In school, I had recovered from the loss of my grandma after months of sincere *du'aa* and crying to Allah at night. My roommate and

I encouraged each other to fast more. I got myself back on track after having a beautiful dream of my grandma. *She is at peace*, I realized. *Alhamdulillah*.

I was back on track, *alhamdulillah*. At this point, we were given the go-ahead to officially have GMSA. It had been such a back-and-forth battle with the school authorities to establish the Muslim Students Association. Remember, I was at a Seventh Day Adventist school, and they had their agenda. Some pastors had tried several times to convert us, but to no avail.

I became the secretary for GMSA. I also ran for President for the Management Department, of which I was a member since its inception. *Alhamdulillah*, at this point, my political agenda was flourishing.

I won and became the President of the Association of Management Studies Students (AMSS), the President of the School of Business Students Association (SOBSA), and I was part of the Special Counsel to the President of the Students Representative Council (SRC). I was also the Secretary and Public relations officer for Ghana Muslim Students Association (GMSA). It was such a busy year. It was also my third year, and classes were getting tougher. I was focusing more on my major (Management) electives at this point.

I was busy with classes and all the extracurricular activities at school. I would come home for the weekend and help my mom at home with washing, cleaning, cooking, etc. There were days where I would be so tired that I would come back to school with my school bag the same way I took it home. *Alhamdulillah*, I was in most of these associations with my roommate, and we both had the same major, so that helped a lot. She helped when she could, and we did most of our studying together.

My roommate and I were each other's keeper. We had each other. When the other girls would go out with guys or when men would stop by with their cars and pick them up, my roommate and I would eat together. If we wanted to go out, we dressed up and went together.

After finals, my roommate and I treated ourselves to a good restaurant. I really cherish my roommate for that. Having that support system really helped, especially in a tempting environment like the university. Today, I think if you do not have a roommate that boosts your *emaan*, you should be part of the Muslim community on your campus. You need that sense of community and belonging, so you are not alone and do not fall into vices.

Life continued and my studies were stressful. I had several corporate meetings. It was as though I was at the epitome of success. I did a summer internship at the Ministry of Information and Media Relations. I got the chance to see the Ministers and attend very important meetings. I wrote memos and reports for different departments under the Ministry. I made a lot of friends and had a very rich network.

It was also around this time that I had formed an NGO called Sadaqa Train to help the poor, needy and orphans. *Alhamdulillah*, it kicked off well.

29

Opening My Heart to Him

I was getting ready to be a senior, my final year at the university. It was 2014 and this was such a "testing" year. My roommate started mounting pressure on me. She used to say, "You are sacking all the men away."

At this point, there were a lot of proposals coming from all corners. I just turned them away by saying, "Please go and speak to my dad." Once you say that, the men have all sorts of excuses, and that was enough for me to know that they were not serious. *If you cannot meet my dad, then you are out,* I thought. *That's the least you could do to be considered.*

There were a couple of good "*da'wah* guys" that wanted my approval first before seeing my dad. "That is not important," I told them. "If you meet my dad and he agrees, I am good. If not, then bye."

At this point, the gentleman who had been pursuing me for almost four years now hardly came to mind most days. For me, the silence from my end would let Sabtiu know that I did not care, hence, he would move on. However, he did not move on. He kept coming and asking.

Now, something started happening. Something started to shift inside of me. Something was changing in my heart. *There must be something he sees in me to put up with my refusals and still come back after all these years*, I thought to myself. I started feeling bad for him. However, I did not want to marry him out of pity. I wanted it to be sincere. If I decided to marry him, I would want to marry him because I could see a future with him and wanted him to be my husband. I couldn't do it for pity, and I couldn't do it for anyone else.

I started plans to hand over the positions I was holding at the time in school. Handing-over ceremonies were planned and executed. Reality started kicking in with plans on what to do after university. I realized I had to make up my mind.

I finished my senior research project in April of 2014, and there were offers here and there for jobs after university. That was when I asked myself, *What next after university?* A voice inside my head said, *Marriage.* I thought to myself, *If you want to stay chaste and keep going, marriage.* This made me reflect. *But to who?* I wondered.

Now, I started making *Istikhaarah*, the special prayer for when you had to decide about something. But there was still bias in it. I would say the dua and think of Sabtiu then say to myself, *Even though this guy is good, not him, because he is in the U.S. Any of the other guys or someone I do not know, just show me a sign.*

I remember hearing at madrasa that you would see a sign in your sleep after you make *Istikhaarah.* I was not seeing any sign, and I was getting restless. My aunt started advising me so hard, reminding me of Sabtiu. She said, "Do you know how many people want their daughters to marry this guy? Two girls are waiting for him to come down and check them out. They are really beautiful."

I was offended when she said that. "Well, I am beautiful too," I said.

She said, "I know, but one of them is light skinned, and you know how some guys get crazy with light skinned ladies."

That put me off. I know my aunt thought that would encourage me to give them a "Yes!" so they could reach out to his people who had been waiting patiently for years for my response. However, that discussion made me madder since I felt belittled.

My aunt realized that her words had backfired, so she used a different tactic. Now, she reminded me of what my grandma had said before her death. "What do you think she would say if she was here?" my aunt asked.

That made me start crying.

"She blessed it before she died," my aunt said. "We want what is good for you."

I cried more.

"What is the matter?" my aunt asked. "You are not telling us anything. What is going on in your head?"

That was when I decided to tell her the truth. "I am scared," I said. "I am scared because he is so good. I am scared that he might just be faking it. I am scared that he'll turn out to be a different person."

That was when she said, "If anyone should be fearful, not you! You are our *malama* (Islamic teacher). You should know better. Once you make up your mind, you should put your trust in Allah."

My mom also had a heart-to-heart with me, and I said to them, "You know what? I will give you all a response this year *inshaaAllah*. It is this year or never."

I realized I had to come clean to Allah. I realized my *Istikhaarah* had been biased thus far. Now, I started making an *Istikhaarah* with an open heart, a sincere one. Then in a dream, I saw him standing behind a tree with a check mark on it. I woke up and said, "This is too good to be true."

Alhamdulillah, just that Friday, I heard a *Khutbah (sermon)* about *Istikhaarah* not literally showing you any sign before you move on. You make the dua and make your decision and rely upon Allah.

Now, Sabtiu and I started having serious discussions. We talked about the future, children's upbringing, where we would live long-term, etc. I started liking him now. *SubhanaAllah!* I realized just when I surrendered fully to Allah, things started falling in place. All this while, it was mind games and my fear, and what people would say that was affecting my decision. Now that I put all of that aside and just spoke to Allah sincerely without any bias, my heart started feeling something else.

I started liking Sabtiu, and I started seeing us having very fruitful discussions. Before, they were very respectful and basic. You know, because it was mainly one way, and I was not interested. Now, I was starting to open up. We talked about parenting, future plans, volunteerism, etc. I was impressed with his train of thoughts. I started realizing he could be the one. I told my mom. I kept her posted.

30

SAYING YES, FINALLY

The Ramadan of that year, 2014, was a life-changing one. I was graduating from the university around the same time. I had told Sabtiu I would give him a response during Ramadan. He remained hopeful. He said, "I know you will be my wife," and for the first time, I answered *yes* inwards. I was shocked. I was happy it did not come out aloud.

At the same time, there was rumor among my circle of friends that one of the *da'wah* brothers liked me and wanted to make a move after Ramadan. This was not a time to be further confused, so I avoided all the voices and input from others.

I told myself, *This Ramadan will be like no other.* I opened my heart, and I threw myself on the prayer mat in the most vulnerable way ever.

I was awake most of the nights praying and crying and begging sincerely for guidance. I remember telling Allah, "If he is the one, I am getting married right after Ramadan. I am not going to drag it out anymore. That is someone's son. He must be serious to stick around for this long."

Sabtiu called my parents and greeted them during Ramadan. I was at home, so he said salaam to me as well. Funny enough, we discussed some Islamic finance research and concluded that working at the bank was not an ideal place for a Muslim due to all the interest/usury-based transactions.

He quit his job before Ramadan but told me later. I was happy about that. He was now jobless. He had saved some money of course, *alhamdulillah*. He started shopping for the *leefe* (traditional clothes for the wife-to-be). I laughed at him. In my head, I was like, *What if I said no? What happens to the clothes?* I told him and he said, "Allah knows best. Allah would do what is best for us."

I was getting ready for my graduation. I was sad because I was not graduating with the sisters I'd started with. They had issues they had to solve, so they could not graduate with us. It hurt me a lot. The day before, I spoke to Sabtiu, and he said his uncle would come to my graduation on his behalf. I laughed thinking he was kidding.

At my graduation, there was an entourage of people. I was speechless. The feeling was priceless. I graduated with a first class. I saw my aunties, uncles, grandpa, mom, dad, sister, brother, cousins,

Daddy's friends, and many others. Sabtiu's uncle was sitting at the back. He said salaam to my family, and my family alerted me that he was there. We took a group picture afterwards, and he left.

I went home after a long day, *alhamdulillah.* I broke my fast, and I remember thinking, *My life is going to start now. I either get married next month or I take the job offers I have waiting in line.* It was as if Allah was telling me, *Don't worry, you will figure it out soon.*

My dad sat me down and started giving me "the talk" (some tough advice) about marriage. It was hard to swallow. I remember he mentioned the *hadith* of the Prophet (peace and blessings be upon him) regarding how one of the things we do not waste time doing was marriage.

"When you love someone, and they love you back, then what are you waiting for?" my dad asked. "Also, when someone good comes to ask for your daughter's hand in marriage, why say no?" he said. "His *deen* is amazing," he told me, speaking of Sabtiu, "and his character is exceptional. He is hardworking also. He has a good background too."

What pierced my heart was when my dad said, "You know, I am passionate about education, and I have given you the best education thus far. You have your Islamic education and your secular education. If Mr. Right was not here, then yes, you can go ahead and pursue your Master's, but if Mr. Right is here and you like him too, then I think you should not delay getting married. Getting married does not stop one from schooling or pursuing further studies."

My dad went on and on about the virtues of marriage, and at this point, I was done. I was convinced. This was my dad, and I loved him. I understood the point he was making.

I felt that I was on track, but I needed Allah's approval now. Everyone around us has approved, and my heart was softening and gradually accepting.

It was the day before *Laylatul Qadr* (during the last ten nights of Ramadan) when Sabtiu arrived to Ghana. He arrived with the intention of getting married. He was so optimistic. He let me know he arrived. I said, "*Alhamdulillah.*"

Sabtiu visited my parents a day afterwards. I was called to come out and see him. I was so shy. I felt like the ground should open so I could enter. I was looking down the entire time. I remember one of the men he'd come with shouting at me, saying, "Won't you raise your head and look at him?" I just smiled. My mom and I walked away after a short while.

At this point, I was ready to say yes. His mannerisms attracted me. He was so humble, and he seemed to be getting along just fine with my dad. *My dad is tough, so if you get along with him, then that is a huge plus.* I did not want it to be as if I was saying yes just because he was there that day. I felt it deep down my heart. I was still not ready to voice it out loud. I waited until the first possible night of *Laylatul Qadr* to feel it.

The first odd night of Ramadan (i.e., the first opportunity for *Laylatul Qadr*) came, and I was standing in prayer. I was sweating, crying, and asking Allah to guide my decision. That was it. I felt it. I said, "If I can get the strength to tell my mom I accept, then indeed this is meant to be." I prayed two *raka'at* (units of prayer) and said the dua for *Istikhaarah.*

I made up my mind and spoke to my mom about agreeing to the *nikaah* (Islamic marriage ceremony). I said, "It will be good to have the *nikaah* in Shawwal, just like our Mother Aisha, *radhiyAllahu'anhaa* (may Allah be pleased with her)." I had always seen myself in Aisha (RA), the most beloved wife of Prophet Muhammad (peace and blessings be upon him) during the latter years of his life and prophethood. She was young, vibrant, fun, intelligent, a virgin, etc.

Sabtiu was informed, and I got the happiest text message ever. I have never seen any text with "*Alhamdulillah*" and "*Allahu Akbar*" that had so many emojis and happiness like his response had.

We immediately started talking about a *nikaah* date. I said, "Any date you give is okay with me."

He said, "Any date, are you sure?"

I said, "Yes!"

He said, "What about a week after Eid?"

I almost choked out of fear. But this time, I was keeping my word. I said, "Yes, *inshaaAllah.*"

I told my mom.

"*Alhamdulillah*," she said. "It's just that, that doesn't give us enough time to shop for your clothes."

Wow! Now, I started getting anxious.

"Don't worry," my mom said. "We will make it happen. We will start shopping tomorrow *inshaaAllah*," she reassured me. "First, let us discuss with Daddy."

My mom had already started the conversation with him so that it would not be awkward for me. *Mothers are the best, aren't they?*

My dad asked, "So what date are you guys thinking about?"

I said, "A week after Eid."

My dad asked, "When exactly?"

"We are thinking the 10th of August."

"And today is…what? The 23rd of July," he said. "*SubhanaAllah!* That is in two weeks? That is soon!"

I almost said, "We will change the date if you want."

As if he was reading my mind, he quickly interjected, "It is all good. Do not change the date. We do not delay marriage," he said. "You want it, right?"

I smiled.

"That is all that matters," he said. "Alright, August 10th it is. I will let the family know."

I thanked him and left.

31

Preparing for My Wedding

Now, the *nikaah* shopping started. It was a stressful week of shopping. It was just around Eid, so everyone was shopping. Word started going out that I was getting married. It spread like a wildfire. We would be shopping, and people would stop my mom and ask, "Is that our bride-to-be? Aww, I am so happy for you my dear." I would look at them and ask my mom how they knew. She'd say, "It spreads like wildfire." I'd say, "Indeed."

Alhamdulillah, we got different fabrics and shoes and bags and jewelries for the occasion. My husband-to-be was an ex-banker, so he decided he would wear suits and, I did not object. I just smiled. I remembered the first time I saw him in suits. It brought back memories that made me tearful. *Allahu Akbar! Look how Allah works. Indeed, Allah is the best of Planners.*

Now that we had the fabrics, we needed a tailor to sew them as soon as possible. With Eid approaching and all the tailors and seamstresses busy, we would need a loyal tailor to do it and do it well. I knew what I wanted. We finally got a professional tailor, but he was a man. I wanted a woman.

I said, "We will work it out."

Because of fighting with tailors in the past, starting from age thirteen, only my cousin who is also a seamstress (female tailor) did my clothes. However, this time, my mom gave her all the other clothes (Super and Holland fabrics) to sew for me to wear as a new bride, so we did not want to burden her with the outfits for the *nikaah* as well.

We got there, and the tailor was introduced to me and my mom. He asked if I had ideas and my mom interjected, "Yes, she does, and she is principled."

"I want a long dress with a turtleneck and long sleeves," I said. "It is a French lace, so I want a thick linen, so my body does not show. However, I want a female to take my measurement. You cannot take my measurement because you are a man."

He said, "Wow! Your mom did not miss her words. You know exactly what you want."

He called one of his apprentices to take my measurement. Instead of thanking him and keeping quiet, I used the opportunity for *da'wah.* He was Muslim by the way. I said, "Why don't you let the ladies that are here take the measurements of the women and girls and you do that of the boys and men, instead of the free mixing and touching people's wives and daughters?"

He was taken aback. I added, "Imagine someone taking your wife's measurement on her shoulders and his hand slipped onto her chest. Would that make you happy?"

My mom smiled and shook her head. The man agreed and said, "I hope she is getting married to a man just like her because we do not have a lot of girls like this. Her husband to be is lucky."

I blushed and my mom felt honored. You could tell from her face. He thanked my mom for bringing me along and took his money to start his work. He promised us he would get it to us the day before the event.

Now, it was about five days to our *nikaah*, and I ran away from home. Well, I ran to my auntie's house. I was feeling overwhelmed, anxious, and nervous. I left WhatsApp and stayed away from social media as much as I could.

Not everyone was happy about the news of my marriage. Some thought it was a lie, and others thought it was a joke. The timing did not make sense to a lot of people. They did not know the back story.

Loved ones wanted enough time to give us a big wedding. My mom sold jewelries and African prints and fabrics, so she had many customers who wanted to honor her. They were trying to convince my mom to talk me into pushing the date further, so they could plan multiple events for me in honor of my mom. I said, "No, no, no!"

I told my mom, "It is my wedding, and we are going to do it as simple as I want it. I do not want any *yaaye* (an agreed outfit for everyone, mostly ladies, at a wedding). I do not want any *yaaye* of any form, and I certainly do not want any party."

We planned our own reception (*waleemah*) for Sunday. We wanted our marriage on a Friday because of the blessings of that day. However, people could not make it and Sunday was the best to get the leaders and everyone else.

A lot of people had ideas and suggestions as to how they thought we should do it. It was getting overwhelming. I knew it was coming from a good place, but I wanted something simple and quiet. Yes, back in the day, I remember saying I would make an announcement on National Television when I am getting married. I pictured a big venue full of people. I was known and my mother was known, so a lot of people would be coming. Now, I just wanted a quiet and a simple *nikaah*. People were not getting it.

I told my mom, "Anyone that calls and says something else, tell them, 'My daughter, the bride-to-be said she doesn't want it.'"

Alhamdulillah, my mom stuck to the plan. A lot of people were upset, however. They wanted more time to plan something bigger and worthier, they thought. I did not want to give anyone time to plan anything I did not want. My fiancé's family too had his sister's and cousins wanting to plan something, some party of some sort, I said no to all of that. I made a lot of enemies then. It was like I was stopping everyone from celebrating my big day.

32

THE BIG DAY

My fiancé and I chose a venue with an army theme, Army Officer's Mess. It was like a barrack or an auditorium for the army officers. It was quite expensive. I loved the army but when I heard the price for the venue, I wanted us to change it. However, my husband-to-be said that has always been his dream *waleemah* venue. He visited that place in 2008 and told himself he would get married there. It was a beautiful venue.

Some previous suitors got mad, and word got to me that, one of the brothers said I could get married on the airplane for all he cared. I smiled. You could smell jealousy in the air, I thought. I had rejected that brother's proposal since high school, so I was not bothered at all by his comment.

It was an intense week. I came back to our house on Thursday evening. I was so nervous. In my mind, we were getting married the next day, Friday. The *mahr* (bride gift) was given from the groom's family to my family, but it had not reached me yet.

I was wearing a sparkly lemon green and gray *abaya.* It was marvelous. I looked good and felt good. I prayed to Allah to bless this union in the heavens. I called my fiancé and told him, "Our *nikaah* has been done in the heavens. I can feel it." He smiled on the phone. "Now, we just have to let the world witness it on Sunday, August 10th."

Nothing much happened at my side on Friday. My family was organizing and preparing the meat and foodstuff to be used for the occasion. I was in the bedroom waiting for my customized hijab to arrive. *Alhamdulillah*, it arrived some minutes after Asr prayer. My clothes for Saturday arrived too, *alhamdulillah.* However, I still did not have my clothes for Sunday ready yet. That was the big day, my *nikaah* day and *waleemah* day.

On Saturday morning, I heard the scream of my old grand auntie singing and calling out my name. I was very nervous. I remained on the prayer mat after Fajr. She called me out, and we went to my grandmother's room.

I was in tears. My grandma would have been the happiest on this day if she were alive. I was told, "Stop crying. Today is the day of joy." My grand auntie, also known as *Taba* (the lady who applies henna on the bride) applied it on my feet, face, and hands. Mostly the *Taba* applies it on the entire body of the bride as well. She knew I wouldn't like that, so she asked me to go to the bathroom and apply it on my body myself. I said, "*Alhamdulillah*." I did that, put on my clothes, and took my seat.

I had to wait several hours for the henna to dry out before taking a shower. I took a shower about two hours later. Now, it was time to dress the bride. I had already agreed that the person to help me dress should be family and they would only help with the hijab and make-up. I would do the rest. My aunt was hired. I dressed up and she came to help with the *gele* (head-piece) and make up.

That was when the fight started. She wanted to put fake eyelashes on me and to shape my eyebrows, but I said, "No!"

She was taken aback. "Your mom told me you would say no, but I did not really think you would say no to my face," she said. "This is your day, and it is a once in a lifetime opportunity. These eyelashes would just be on for an hour. It is a temporary one, just for today."

I said, "No."

She said, "Okay, let me shape your eyebrows."

I said, "No."

She said, "Okay, let me style your hair"

"No," I said. "I am wearing the hijab and you can put the *gele* on top of the hijab."

She got mad and called one of my aunties. She came and was about to start convincing me, but I snapped. "I am not doing anything to please anyone," she said. "I will only do what I believe is right."

My aunt came in and started throwing insinuations here and there. She said, "Even the daughter of scholars put on eyelashes on their wedding day. What do you want to show us? What haven't we seen before? It is just for a few hours."

I said, "No."

"Okay, she is leaving," my aunt said.

"Do you know how many people have booked me today? There are two big weddings that have booked me, but I told them I cannot be there because my daughter is getting married. Now that I want to make you look good, this is what I get? I am leaving."

I said, "Okay."

After going back and forth with my other aunties, she left and sent her apprentice to me. The apprentice came and before she started, I told her my conditions. She said, "I have already heard about you from your aunt on the phone."

"Good," I said. "Let us do this. If this is going to bring stress on everyone, I will just stay indoors. It is my wedding and I think I should have a say."

She gave in and helped me fix my hijab and we put the *gele* on top of the hijab. *Alhamdulillah*, with a little make up and no fake eyelashes and fake eyebrows, I was ready to come out of the room.

I came out to greet the womenfolk, as is customary when you do not have a big party. I was led by my bridesmaid, Kabira, and my over-the-top auntie, Yabash. I love her. She is that over-the-top auntie who respected my boundaries. We have an amazing relationship. She likes to do all sort of things that I do not agree with, but we respect each other.

I greeted the women in and outside the house, and I was taken to my mom. The entire time I was reciting *Ayatul Kursi* because some faces were too gloomy, and some were happy. Some people were straight out jealous. They checked me out from top to bottom. I was looking flawless, *maashaaAllah*. You could hear some people whispering among themselves: "Why is she fully covered even though it is just us women?"

I changed several times and did the same routine. *Alhamdulillah*, the day ended by Maghrib, and I prayed my Salah and hung out with some sisters. I remember Mariam Khidr, Khairat and Hawa of course. That night, I could barely sleep. Tomorrow was the big day in the sight of everyone.

Sunday morning arrived, I prayed Fajr and did all my *dhikr*. I wore a white cloth as is customary for a bride on a Sunday morning before the *nikaah*. At about 8:00 a.m., I was told to go and change. Mostly, there are people or a person that helps the bride change, but I canceled that for myself. I only needed help with the make-up and hijab. I dressed myself.

I remember seeing my dad in his white outfit, and he was looking so happy and joyful. He asked me if I would be reciting Qur'an at the masjid, as he overheard some people saying I might do so to show that I have completed the recitation of the Qur'an.

"No," I said. "I do not have to prove a point to anyone. People do it and no offense to them, but it is not for me."

"Alright, whatever makes you comfortable," my dad said. "See you at the masjid." Then he left.

I dressed up in all white. That outfit arrived that morning. *SubhanaAllah!* I remember the scene like it was just yesterday. It was a long white blouse with a long skirt all the way to the floor. My hijab was a customized hijab with gray sparkles all over it. It was beautiful. I looked marvelous and fabulous. I felt good. I was ready for this. It had been such a long road.

Alhamdulillah, we got to the masjid and the *nikaah* was contracted by the Imam. He announced my *mahr* and asked both sides, and we all answered in affirmation. My husband was over the moon. He kept saying, "*Allahu Akbar! Allahu Akbar!*" My dad's eyes were filled with tears. It was such a priceless moment.

It had been so long. My entire life I wanted to make my dad proud. This was the day I felt I made him the proudest, *Alhamdulillah.*

After the *nikaah* was done, we then got ready for the reception in the afternoon. Of course, my "mothers" (i.e., aunties and other mothers in the community) had to do their own thing. I was tossed between my in-law's house and our house greeting and visiting people. Some friends also visited after Dhuhr, and we had an amazing chat.

My aunties and mothers were singing and clapping. It was beautiful. I was placed in the middle, and they surrounded me, singing, and clapping. It was a day filled with joy and laughter.

But I was fasting. I did not want to eat anything. I wanted it to be a day that Allah would look at me with a lot of mercy, so I decided to fast. The beautiful thing was that my bridesmaid, Kabirah, decided to fast too.

33

OUR WALEEMAH

We finally got ready and arrived at our reception venue, Army Officers Mess. *MaashaaAllah*, it was beautiful, and people were waiting. I felt bad because we put 2:30 p.m. on the flyer but arrived at 4:00 p.m. due to matters that were out of our control. *Alhamdulillah*, people still waited.

Our *waleemah* (wedding reception) was beautiful and wonderful. Men were on one side and the women on another side. There were sisters ushering sisters to their seats, and brothers ushering brothers to their seats. There were army officers too in eyesight, so no one could mess around.

Our reception was amazing. It was filled with Qur'an recitation, lectures on getting married and staying married, poetry that was customized by Ayuba Hud, a rising poet, and a drama/play by One Ghana Production. It was fun filled.

As we were sitting at our table, I could see all the people, some busy taking pictures of us and, others were busy counting the balloons and flowers. There were sisters at the back making sure the large crowd got food. There was so much to eat.

Maghrib was approaching, and the day was wrapped up. People wanted pictures from all corners. I was pulled here and there. I forgot that I was fasting. My bridesmaid, Kabira, took some water and broke her fast. It was after 25 minutes of dragging me here and there that I finally got some water to break my fast with.

Some sisters were upset and started asking why I fasted on my *nikaah* day. How do I tell them it was a personal decision? I was not ready to explain myself in the crowd. I just smiled and kept it going. We wanted a place to pray, but my people were dragging me to enter the car and go home. *Alhamdulillah*, I was brought home and I quickly prayed.

After I prayed Maghrib, it was *'Ishaa* shortly thereafter. I prayed *'Ishaa*. I was ready to pray Witr when my beloved Mama Saya, my uncle's wife, who was like my second mom in the house said, "You can pray your Witr in your husband's house."

The lights were off. Before arriving to the house, I prayed for forgiveness for whatever went wrong at the ceremony, and I asked

Allah to show me a sign if he had accepted and approved this marriage. I got home, and as we approached to park the car; the lights went off. I smiled.

I remember my aunt, Mama Aboni saying, "Nana, the lights are off."

I said, "I can see that, no problem. I'm happy." That was the sign I wanted. The lights were off, and the enemies would not be able to see me walk out of the door to my husband's house.

My mom gave me her blessings and wished me the best. She was crying and I could feel it. I started crying too. My aunt, my father's sister, made me weep when she said, "Grandma would have been so proud of you if she were alive."

I started weeping bitterly now. Memories of my last moments with my grandma flooded my mind. This was the house that I had lived in for the past twenty-one years. This was the house I knew, the parents I lived with and the aunties, uncles, and cousins I grew up with.

My dad was chitchatting with my uncles outside the house. I said, "*Assalaamu Alaikum*" to them and left. It was so emotional. The women started singing as I entered the *trotro* (public transportation) to be taken to my in-laws. It was an emotional night. The lights were back on our way there, and I could see the familiar places and corners of the neighborhood I was used to. *Now, I am starting a whole new life with a new person that was brought up differently than I was.*

We arrived at my in-laws, and my family and my in-laws exchanged a few pieces of advice and my family left. Reality kicked in quickly. I was very hungry, but I could not ask anyone for food. I was left to myself. No one said anything to me. I was covered with a big scarf.

I reached out to my phone. *Should I call my husband to come and get me?* I did not know what was planned. I waited until after 10:00 p.m. before my husband arrived. Now, it was another hour drive to our new home.

We finally arrived. *Alhamdulillah*, we performed *wudhoo'* and prayed our Sunnah. He put his hands on my forehead and said the prayer for newlyweds, and I excitedly thought, *Yes! He passed this test too.* Our married life started.

PART FOUR

BECOMING A WIFE AND MOTHER

"I hope I am more kind, patient, mindful, and forgiving than any previous days' version."
—Eric Overby, *Legacy*

34

Newly Married

We enjoyed our first week as a couple. The only annoying thing were the people who kept calling early in the morning. *For Allah's sake, I just got married. Can I get a break?* I also disliked people visiting. *At least, give me some breathing space.* People kept calling and asking details about my wedding, like, "How much was the venue?" "Who did the decoration?" "How much was your outfit?" "Who was the tailor?" And all these calls at 7:00 a.m. in the morning. People were visiting from all over, literally just days after marriage. I was so upset inside, but I was holding it in.

My sincere advice for visiting a newlywed is to please give them some space to enjoy without interruption. Come on! No visiting for at least some weeks or a week at least. They need some time to settle down and get used to each other.

Long story short, we had a hectic first few weeks of marriage and decided to move to New York to continue living. We arrived in New York City and the first few days were amazing. Memories of some familiar places flooded my head. We walked and held hands and were so much in love. You know that feeling of newlyweds. You know you cannot have enough of each other. You always want to be together and do everything together. *Alhamdulillah*, it was lovely.

Reality set in after a couple of months. My husband was jobless. No one knew this except me. Allah had seen us through this far. *Now, what do we do?* We started looking for a job together. We would walk for a long time, from office to office dropping applications here and there. I was optimistic.

I remember we got tired and stopped at Dunkin Donuts one day. All we had was $5. I bought two chocolate chip cookies and he just had water. His eyes were fixated on me, and I was just enjoying the cookies bashfully. Anyone who saw us knew we were newlyweds. We were so much in love.

A week passed by, and we did not hear from any of the jobs we applied to. He went out and took a cashier job at a retail store even though he had two degrees at this point. He did not tell me the details, but I just knew the job was downtown. I think he did not want me to feel bad for him.

I now remembered the advice some women gave me the night I was leaving my parents' home. They said, "Patience, patience, and may Allah give you what to eat." That time, I thought that was silly. *You work hard and get what you want. How do you expect Allah to feed you? Do you want Allah to come down and feed you?* I did not understand that statement on a higher level. Times were getting hard now. *Alhamdulillah*, his first paycheck from this new job came, and we did some grocery shopping and stocked the kitchen. We started living good again, *alhamdulillah.*

It was a few weeks before Eid-ul-Adha. His boss was Asian. My husband asked for the day off. Apparently, that was not okay since it was a busy day on that day. His boss was hesitant. He told me, and I said I would meet the boss and speak to him. We went together but the boss realized how curious I was about the business and how quickly I was reading the items and taking note of things.

He paused our discussion and asked, "Do you want to give it a try?"

I said, "Why not?"

He trained me for a few minutes, and I got it. I got a job on the spot. I became a cashier for the smaller retail store, and my husband was a cashier for the bigger store. He liked us both.

On day two, he said, "I think you are better than your husband, so I might switch you."

"No!" I said. "I have been in America before, that is why my English sounds better"

My husband still had his Ghanaian accent and was not as extroverted as I was. The customers liked me. The following week was Eid-ul-Adha, and I brought it up again. Our boss was not thrilled about us taking off during that time. He said, "Then one of you should be here, and the other goes." I was not comfortable with that reply. Since the job was new and we both enjoyed it, he threatened us. He said, "You either come on Eid day, or you quit for good."

I said, "I don't think it has come to that."

He said, "I like you and your husband, and you are a newly married couple. You need this job so you can stand on your feet. What would one day of missing prayers do to you?"

Mind you, we had been pausing to pray Dhuhr and Asr during work time, and he was not happy about that either. But he could not do anything since we spread out our lunch break for that.

We came home and talked about it. My beloved husband said, "This is a test from Allah. Let us keep convincing him and see if he changes his mind. If not, then we will have to quit since our Eid day is more important than the job."

We were ready to come the following day and make up for that day, but this man was insistent that we come on Eid day, as that was his busiest day. We talked to him the day before Eid, and he was still not budging.

We came home and smiled at each other. My husband said to me, "We have done it before, and we will do it again. We will go for Eid tomorrow and if he does not take us back, then we will quit, and Allah would provide."

We had an amazing first Eid together. I was introduced to the community and at this time, I had started volunteering at the madrasa where my husband taught on the weekend.

He called my husband right after the Eid prayer around 10:00 a.m. and asked where he was. My husband said we were at Eid. Our boss told him, "That's it. Then you should not come back to work." He fired him. My husband smiled and told me, "Allah will provide."

The subsequent weeks were tough, but Allah always has your back when you trust in Him. We were still job hunting. I would send in applications online for him while he went in person from office to office, every single day.

Alhamdulillah, people in the community were visiting and giving us gifts, and that was what we lived on. Allah works in mysterious ways. No one knew we were struggling to make ends meet. We heard about a big new supermarket that was opened by a rich African. We decided to give it a try after madrasa one Sunday.

Of course, my big mouth started mentioning the names of the foodstuff I saw. My husband introduced himself to the boss and the boss said, "I hope she is the one coming and not you." That was kind of cold, but the boss quickly smiled and said, "I know you do not do this kind of job, my brother."

The boss gave me a few lessons and asked me to go around the shop and memorize some foreign vegetable names and their prices. I did that and came back in a few minutes. He told my husband to bring me the following day to train for an hour or thirty minutes since I was a smart lady. If he was impressed, I could start working straight away.

Alhamdulillah, my husband dropped me off the next day and went job hunting. I trained for less than thirty minutes and worked for two hours. The boss was impressed. He worked out my schedule and I told him I teach on the weekend so that was out. I got Tuesday to Friday, with Friday schedule being after Jumu'ah prayers. It was a good schedule.

Alhamdulillah, I started working and I would come home and see my husband so sad. It hurt him that I was working, and he was not. No one knew this. He was getting frustrated at this point. He attended a lot of training and orientations, but nothing came out of it.

At one point, Sabtiu even took a sales job with Verizon. However, it was commission based and he had to go door to door to convince people to use Verizon. Once he got a person signed up, he got commission for that after a week of the person using their services.

He would come home tired from all the walking and knocking on people's doors. One day, Sabtiu told me about a person screaming at him and cursing at him when he knocked at their door after the person opened to find out that he was a salesperson from Verizon.

I felt so bad for him. He was tired at this point. I told him, "Don't worry. You should continue making calls and sending applications online." He did that, and I went to work every week at the supermarket.

Alhamdulillah, we would recite Qur'an together after Fajr, and eat breakfast together. I would make his lunch before leaving for work. I made sure I started dinner prep before leaving as well. Sometimes, I made dinner and at other times, Sabtiu did. I would come home, and he would calm me down and sympathize with me. As a cashier, I stood for six to eight hours a day, and it was hard. Some days were better than others. I would recite Qur'an on the bus during the commute and would start singing *nasheeds* when I was feeling down.

Sabtiu really felt that he let me down. I comforted him and said, "Allah has His plans."

He promised me, "Once I start working, you do not have to work."

I knew him, and I believed him. Our relationship was going strong, and we were there for each other.

35

Newly Pregnant

Some months later, I started feeling sick. I did not know what was wrong, but I was throwing up. With everything that was going on, I stopped thinking about getting pregnant. However, I went for a checkup, only to find out that I was pregnant. I was excited and nervous. I was told to come in two weeks for an ultrasound to know exactly how far I was.

I came for that appointment, and I was told I was several weeks in. However, this was a critical stage where a lot of women have miscarriages if they do so much hard work. I said I was a cashier, and the doctor said it was not advisable. If my boss would allow me to sit, then that would be helpful. Otherwise, she would advise me to get another job or stay home until the pregnancy was solid and firm.

My mind was on fire. I was the one bringing in income at this point. *If I stop, what will we eat? How will we pay our rent? Phone bills? Utility bills, etc.?* I discussed it with my husband, and he said, "We will do what is best for you." He suggested that I explain my situation to my boss.

I went to work and told my boss that I need to sit while working. I did not tell him the reason, but I said, "I am not feeling well."

He said, "You can take the day off and come tomorrow." He was not understanding.

I said, "I can manage."

I brought a chair and sat, as the register was not busy. He was not happy and said this would undermine my job, so I took the chair back.

I started taking longer than the five-minute break I usually took to pray. The bathroom was in the basement, and I used to be very fast, running and carrying heavy things out of the way to get to the bathroom to make *wudhoo'* and pray. Now, I needed to be careful, so I could not do much.

My boss started complaining that I stay long in my *Salah* and that I spend so much time in the bathroom.

I explained, "I'm pregnant."

"Oh okay," he said. "Then it means you will stop working, right?"

I thought about it. I wanted to say yes, but I remembered my situation at home and felt pity for my already stressed-out husband. I said, "No, I will work for a little bit more."

My boss started giving me more tasks to do. It was like a deliberate attempt to make me stressed out. He would give me and the other cashiers so much stuff to stack at the register, at the bottom and on top. It hurt my back a lot.

When I complained, he said, "There's nothing I can do." I cried a lot. He teased me and said, "You have a big heart." I did not know what that meant then.

I was sick the following day and was rushed to the doctor's office. I was throwing up badly, and I was diagnosed with Hyperemesis Gravidarum. My doctor advised that I quit my job. I texted my boss and said that I could not come to work that day. He got mad and hung up after he called to confirm what I had texted him.

I discussed it with my husband, and he said, "You have to quit." So, I quit my job. We were both jobless at this point, and I was pregnant.

We went for madrasa on the weekend, and I remember praying in *sujood* to Allah to make a way out for us. My husband went to different restaurants the following Monday and volunteered to do any *halal* job they had there. He served as a waiter, just to provide for me and our unborn baby. He came home saying, "I got this job."

I felt so bad for him. How can a person with two degrees work as a waiter in America? I could not wrap my head around it. The following months were tough. I threw up a lot and was sick most of the time. I will talk more about my pregnancy journey in the next chapter.

I have not worked since. Sabtiu fulfilled his promise, and I could not love him more. He is the real deal. I love him for walking the talk. I love him for making me enjoy staying at home and doing me. I love being a wife, a full-time wife.

36

Trials of Pregnancy

Pregnancy! That word scares me. It includes my most delicate moments in my marital journey. A time in a woman's life when she cannot manage herself? *SubhanaAllah!* It was one thing hearing that pregnant women go through a lot and throw up a lot. When you are the one that is pregnant, it is a whole different ball game.

As I mentioned, I was diagnosed with Hyperemesis Gravidarum in my first pregnancy. This is a condition that makes one very sick. Emesis Gravidarum is a fancy name for *morning sickness*. Add *hyper* to it and you get Hyperemesis Gravidarum, meaning extreme morning sickness. Some people call it a disorder, others call it a sickness. I call it a condition. My midwife said it happens to about 2% of pregnant women. It is rare.

My pregnancy life was tough but beautiful. This was our first baby. My husband was very supportive and helpful. I threw up a lot and lost a lot of weight. At about nineteen weeks, I lost so much weight that the doctor almost hospitalized me. I begged her not to hospitalize me and promised I would work on it. I asked her to give me one more week. I told her I would gain the needed weight.

I informed Sabtiu, and he was so concerned. I started eating fearlessly. However, I would eat and throw up. I would eat again and throw up, and the cycle continued. I was motivated to eat even though I was throwing up a lot.

Alhamdulillah, I went for the next appointment, and my doctor said I had gained a little bit and if I continue like that, there would be no need to hospitalize me. I was so happy that I called my husband instantly and informed him.

All this while, no one in my birth family knew that I was pregnant except my mom. However, she only knew that I was pregnant. She did not know that I was going through a lot of pain. Friends and family were leaving messages here and there, and I could not respond. Some people even insinuated that I had forgotten about them because I now lived in America.

Some of the messages made me cry, and others made me sad. If only they knew what I was going through. I was mostly lying on the floor or in front of the toilet. I would throw up so much that my eyes were teary. I would throw up from my nose and my mouth. It was worse when I ate rice.

I continued to throw up from my nose and mouth, and I would cry a lot. I was in a lot of pain. I could not sleep. I was mostly awake. I would try my hardest to make some dinner for my husband. Sometimes, I could not. I would just make oatmeal because it had no smell. The smell of the food irritated me a lot.

Sabtiu was loving and very understanding. There were times he would come back from work late and hungry, but there was no food. I would feel so bad for him. However, I was restless and just lying on the floor.

I could not manage myself. My hair was all over the place. I could not style it like I used to. I had no strength for anything. I would just pray, try to eat something, shower and watch TV. I would also listen to lectures or try to find something funny to make me laugh and forget my condition.

My cravings were increasing. I remember my husband came home one evening and I was craving for Banku and Okro soup with fish. Mind you, I am not a fish fan, but that was what I wanted to eat. He instantly changed his clothes, prayed Maghrib and took a cab to the African restaurant. Once he brought it and I tried it, I did not like it. The garlic was too much. I could not complain. I was forcing myself to eat. He was encouraging me to eat. He was so supportive.

The following day I was craving Omo Tuo and groundnut soup. He got that too for me, but the garlic was too much again. I managed to eat it. I threw up shortly afterwards. I would toss and turn at night, rolling from one side of the bed to the other. He would see me in a lot of pain. He would make *dua* for me when he woke up to pray *Tahajjud (late-night prayer).* He would rub my belly and pray for me. We were so in love with this baby that we had not met yet.

At madrasa, somehow, Allah gave me a lot of strength. I would teach and move around like nobody's business. I was literally strong at the masjid, so I loved the weekend because of that. Also, the students were very supportive and helpful. They would get me water or a chair to sit on to pray my Salah. They would always ask me if I needed something. Sometimes they would ask to touch and rub my belly.

Day by day, I was getting bigger and bigger. Different medications were given, and gradually, my excessive vomiting reduced. Now, I could eat a lot. The remaining months were full of eating. It was as if I was making up for all the food I had not eaten in the past six months. I would eat and eat and eat. I loved spicy food. Everything had to have some pepper in it. Even bread and eggs were with kpakposhito (hot/Jamaican pepper).

One night, my husband came back from work, and I was craving for some pizza. Before he got home, I had searched the whole house for money and got only $2. I was waiting for him to give me some more. He got home, and I was so excited. We prayed and I served him some food. I did not want to eat what I made.

After he finished eating, I smiled and asked, "Can I have pizza?" He started touching his pockets and looked worried. I was like, "I have $2, I just need $3."

He said, "Yes, but I do not have money."

I asked, "How? But you are working."

"I paid the bills before coming to the house," he said.

I was disappointed. He looked worried. I was very hungry. I went to the kitchen and drank water. He was busily searching the house and his clothes for any money, but he could not find any. He went to the coins jar, and he was shocked that there were only pennies there. I told him that was where I got the $2 from.

I felt bad that he was super worried. I remembered there was a pizza place that sold a pizza slice for $1 ten minutes away from our building. I said, let us take a walk together. He was in his gray *thobe*, and I was in my cream jilbab, and my tummy was very big. We took a walk and were cracking jokes. I felt so good and relaxed. I bought the two slices of pizza for $2, and we walked back home.

Alhamdulillah, we had some apple juice in the fridge. I got some and ate the pizza with it. I was so full. I felt good. He was happy that I was all smiles and laughing. We prayed *'Ishaa* and he made dua and rubbed my belly. That was my favorite part, him rubbing my belly and making dua for our unborn child.

Alhamdulillah, the subsequent weeks were spent shopping for baby clothes. We shopped and shopped and had a lot of stuff. You know that first baby lacks nothing. New parents go overboard and shop a lot because they never know what to expect. We were no exception.

I walked a lot, every day for about thirty to forty-five minutes. People in the neighborhood would stop me and pray for me. Everyone kind of knew me by now because of my daily walks. I thought labor would be easy because I was active.

37

GIVING BIRTH

Alhamdulillah, after a rough final week of pregnancy I felt as though my water broke. Sabtiu came from work, and I said, "I think my water broke." He quickly prayed and we rushed to the hospital. I got there and I was only two centimeters dilated, so I was sent back home. The following day, I was in a lot of pain, and we returned. I was three and half centimeters dilated by now. They admitted me.

The long road of labor started. It was tough. I was in a lot of pain. It was as though a dozen people were hitting my waist with different axes at the same time. I was so heavy and big. Most people thought I was having twins. My husband and I were saying lots of *duas*. We said all the *duas* we knew, and I was still not far along yet. The poor guy started dozing off.

All this while, my mom was on the other side of the world in Africa and could not sleep. She was on the phone asking for updates and sending her *duas*. Sabtiu fell asleep in the chair next to my bed. Can you blame him? He had a tired day at work and now was stuck with me for hours at the hospital.

I refused any pain medication. I said, "I am the daughter of my mother." She had all of us naturally, and I wanted to have my child naturally with no help. So, I refused any pain medication. My midwife was understanding.

I was in a lot of pain and got to eight centimeters now. I was told the baby would come out when I was ten centimeters dilated. The next two centimeters felt like forever. I was eight centimeters for over two hours. I had lost all my energy now.

Of course, they refused to give me water. I did not drink water for the past twelve hours. I only had two cups of ice cubes. I was really thirsty. That was when flashes and stories of the dead started flooding my mind. I started thinking I might die due to the immense pain.

I started saying the Shahada, "*Laa ilaaha illaAllah*" (*None has the right to be worshipped except Allah alone*). Not long after, I was nine and half centimeters. I was told, "You can start pushing now." Sabtiu asked me to continue saying the Shahada.

All the nurses were encouraging. They said, "We do not know what that means, but it is working." However, I could not say it out loud anymore. I was saying it in my head. I asked my husband to say it. The other nurse and the midwife joined in. The room was in chorus and symphony of "*Laa ilaaha illaAllah.*"

After a couple of tries, I pushed this big baby boy out by the help of Allah. My husband was in joy and shaking. He was confused. He stood there motionless. I called out to him to cut the umbilical cord. I received my baby with *Allahu Akbar!* My husband ignored the nurse and called the *azan* before going to her and cutting the umbilical cord. Our baby was flawless. Every baby is perfect, aren't they? *Alhamdulillah.*

The birth of my son brought a lot of happiness and tests to our marriage. The early days were tough for me due to the sleepless nights. My husband also got a better job with a company whose CEO and his wife were both Muslims. Sabtiu was able to go for Jumu'ah without worrying about beating the time because his boss was at Jumu'ah with him.

His boss's wife loved me like a daughter. We were like one big family. I loved her like my mom. She would send me different kinds of fish and I would make all kinds of food for Sabtiu to send to work and share with them all for lunch.

You see, we were tested with a tough year, but the year that followed was calm and easy. When Allah *Subhanan Wa Ta'alaa* tells us in the Qur'an that, "Verily, with difficulty comes ease," believe it! This was our ease, *alhamdulillah*.

38

My Second Pregnancy

You would think with the first pregnancy, I was experienced right? Oh No! Two years later, I was pregnant again, and this time, it was more difficult than the first. I had Hyperemesis Gravidarum again. It was way worse than before. Not only was I sick, but I lost interest in everything. I was studying for my Diploma in Islamic Studies and barely finished. *Alhamdulillah*, I pulled through and put that on the side.

Just after completing my studies, my symptoms got worse. I had hot flushes, and my feet were like they were on fire when I went to bed. Most of the time, I was moody. I had several migraines. I could not really get any strong medication because of the pregnancy. It was mostly Benadryl or Tylenol. I was so upset.

This time, my husband was not as supportive. Work took most of his time, and he was not as helpful at home. Sabtiu thought this was my second pregnancy so I should be experienced by now. It was as if I was speaking to the wall when I tried explaining to him how I was feeling. He was not getting it and was not sympathetic. He thought he gave me heaven because I was at home and did not have to go to work. "Why are you complaining?" he'd ask.

I know that sounds logical, right? It was not that simple. I had a toddler who was very active. I was nurturing him, homeschooling him, managing the home and cooking every day. My husband never ate outside. It was like stabbing him when you'd ask for something outside the home. *Wasn't this the same man who cared for me and bought me stuff in my first pregnancy?* I expected more if not same. I did not even get half of the treatment I received with my first pregnancy. I was upset. I was sad and gradually started resenting Sabtiu.

What made it worse was when I went for my appointment complaining of my condition (Hyperemesis Gravidarum) and my midwife said, "There is nothing anyone or I can do. This condition is still being researched and we might use your experiences to further enhance the research. We do not know the cause, and it mostly is genetic for now." I got angry.

Nothing and no one was making it easy for me. There was no one to ask for help. My husband refused to let me ask for help from sisters in the community. I was feeling helpless. I would throw up at the hospital, on the way to the hospital and at home.

My husband could barely stand me. He did not want to go places with me. I would need to use the bathroom every fifteen to thirty minutes. I could not walk fast. Sabtiu would not say a word, but the look he would give me made me feel like vanishing. I figured the best option at this point was to avoid any outing with him. He welcomed it.

I focused my energy on my son. He would laugh and make me happy. He was learning the Arabic alphabets at this point. He was there to smile and make me laugh. He would eat whatever I made with no complaints. I was trying my best to cook with a condition which worsened while I cook.

Repeatedly, I would hear from my midwife, "Get someone to do the cooking for you. You are not supposed to be cooking."

I got mad one day and shouted at her. "I am here alone, and I have no one! It is just my husband, my son and me. We have no family here. I have no option than to cook for myself and my family."

She snapped back, "Well, then your husband should be helping with the cooking."

It was also at this time that my husband started a second job with a colleague who was not that much of a good influence. Sabtiu would come home and say things that would make me really upset. However, I kept silent. This colleague, with his other single friends, would say things like, "Do not help your wife too much, or else she will take you for granted" or "Once they are home, they have to do everything. Why should I eat outside when I have a wife?" It was as if my husband was not seeing and hearing me. I was in tears most of the time.

I was that "perfect wife" who would keep the house in order, cook different meals, educate my son, and welcome my husband. Pregnancy coupled with HG made me helpless and unmanageable. I thought my husband would understand since he lived with me and knew my condition more than anyone else. To him, I was just exaggerating and making things up.

He annoyed me one day by saying, "I read too, you know. You must be active and move around more. Sitting at one place for a long time will not help you."

I felt like throwing the plate at him that day. "You barely help with nothing and there are dishes in the sink," I said, "and you are telling me this while I am trying to eat breakfast at 11:00 a.m.?" I looked at him, and I think he understood the look.

Anytime he walked out of that door, I was anxious as to what he was coming home with. I didn't know what his so-called friends would tell him this time. I disliked them with each passing day even though I had not met them.

I lost interest in overworking myself and trying to please my husband at my expense. I would be cooking and pausing to throw up because of the smell of the food. He would just be sitting there. I had enough and started to cook only when I could. That irked him. He was not excited about eating leftovers.

One day, I said I wanted something from the restaurant, and he refused to go get it. I said, "Okay." I ate whatever we had. I started cooking simple meals that did not have much smell, like Tuo Zafi and Kuuka and the likes. He would eat sometimes and other times, he would just have Cereal.

One day I cried so hard, it got to him. He got up and got me food from the restaurant. His demeanor and the negative things that were said after getting the food could have stopped me from eating, but I ignored it and pretended not to hear him.

You know, what most men do not know is that *pregnancy is very difficult, and each pregnancy is different.* I was gradually becoming an expert at my condition (HG). I would recommend what the midwife should give to me. I realized she was not as educated on the condition as my previous midwife was, so I asked to go back to my previous midwife and continue the pregnancy journey with her. She understood and was empathetic.

Abby, my first midwife would give me all this consoling advice and things to do to help. Most worked and some did not. I took the remaining months into my hands. I would wake up and see my son and give him a hug. My husband and I were drifting. He was getting tired of me and did not know how to handle everything that I was going through. It was too much for him. He was working double shifts and staying out a lot to avoid me.

Initially, I cried when this started, but I quickly realized that his schedule and avoidance could work to my advantage. I did not have to worry about dinner. I would eat anything I could make, and my son was still breastfeeding and eating. Some people advised me to stop breastfeeding since that might be affecting me too. Breastfeeding made me feel better because of the attachment and closeness I felt with my son. I consulted with my midwife, and she said I could continue since I was not in any pain.

I continued and played with my son a lot. I would teach him, and we would roll on the floor together. He loved his mama. We were so close. We did everything together. I would tell him stories and he would laugh and make his silly comments here and there. Before Daddy arrived, we would be in bed for the most part. Sabtiu helped himself with whatever was there, and I could hear him open the fridge from the bedroom.

I would wake up and pee like eight times in the night, and my son would be right there with me. My husband would be sleeping. Sometimes, I would try to hold my vomit, so I did not wake anyone up. I would turn on the shower as I vomited so my son would think I was taking a shower. He would walk to the bathroom door and knock, "Mommy, mommy!" I would drag myself on the floor and open the door for him. My son would wipe my tears and clean my vomit with his hands. He would give me a hug and kiss my forehead. My son loved his mama. It was beautiful.

39

Pregnancy Trials

Alhamdulillah, Ramadan was quickly approaching, and I had a lot of resentment towards my husband by then. However, I knew I had to forgive him so Allah would forgive me. I came forward and voiced certain things to Sabtiu. We talked about it, and he agreed to be better.

I suggested a trip away from home, and we took a trip to Atlanta, Georgia. It was beautiful and refreshing. The family we stayed with sympathized with me. She was shocked that I was still throwing up at about eight months pregnant. She told my husband, "Please care for her, as this is not normal."

I said, "This is how the other pregnancy was too. However, this is just worse, as my vomit reduced to about twice a day after seven months with my first pregnancy. However, I'm eight months pregnant and still throwing up about four to five times a day."

Our relationship got better after the trip. I suffered a lot of infections soon after coming back home. I had an ear infection, eye infection, false contractions, sleepless nights, and the non-stop bathroom visits.

SubhanaAllah! Something interesting happened. I was way overdue at this point. Some nurses suggested I eat some hot pepper, others said I should do a lot of squats, Kegel exercises, etc. I did everything, but the baby was not ready to come out. I prayed about it, and I had a feeling baby would come out on Friday *inshaaAllah.*

On Friday, I was in a lot of pain. I took my hospital bag from the closet and placed it on the couch. I was in a lot of pain. This pain was familiar. Contractions had started. I gradually woke up and took a shower before Fajr. I was in a lot of pain. I sat and prayed Fajr. I was smiling on the couch.

My husband asked, "Are you okay?"

I said, "This baby will come out today *inshaaAllah.*"

He smiled and walked away. After watching him recite the Qur'an, I went back to sleep. It was 7:00 a.m. and I was still in a lot of pain. I decided to wait and give my son a shower first. He was still sleeping. The pain continued. I reached out to him and woke him up. I gave him a shower and gave him breakfast. I left my husband's breakfast in the kitchen. Sabtiu was still sleeping since it was his day off from work.

Funny enough, I did not eat anything. At this point, the pain was immense. I told my husband I could not handle it anymore. He was about to call the cab (taxi) when I said I would walk to the hospital, as it would help in pushing. I told him to bring my hospital bag later. I wore my black jilbab and took my purse with my phone, dates, insurance card and small hijab in it. I walked slowly with contractions in between.

I finally got to the hospital. At the door, a lady rushed and shouted, "She is in labor! Call the emergency! Look at how she is sweating and in pain!"

I waved dismissively and said, "I am okay."

She insisted. The emergency staff came and asked to put me on the bed to enter the elevator and go to the labor floor. I told them, "I am okay. You should leave me alone."

This lady insisted. She was a sweet African sister.

I said, "No!"

She said, "Okay, at least, let us walk with you."

They opened the doors for us, and I registered and entered the elevator with them all. We arrived at the labor ward, and she explained to them that she saw me in pain in front of the hospital and shouted for help.

I said, "I was just resting because I have been walking for thirty minutes."

The receptionist, sensing pain and danger, rushed me to triage and I was asked to change into labor clothes. I kept screaming, "I want only women, no man allowed!"

They said, "We will do what you want."

I said, "Please call my midwife and ask for my birth plan. I want only females, and I mean it." Boy, did they mean it? I was checked in, and I was six centimeters dilated already.

The midwife available asked me to walk some more, saying, "This baby will come before we realize."

With paperwork and everything, it was almost 12:00 noon. I called Sabtiu and updated him. He quickly rushed to the hospital with my bag and then left for Jumu'ah. My husband was at *Jumu'ah* Salah (Friday prayer) when I was ten centimeters dilated and ready to push. I did not want him to miss the birth of his son. My midwife asked me to call him. I said, "He is at Jumu'ah and can't speak."

She was shocked and horrified. "Wait, what?" she said. "You are in labor, and your husband cannot leave the mosque to come and help you? He can if it is *urgent*."

I said, "Today, Friday, is a special prayer. He is listening to the sermon, and he cannot speak. He will be done soon. I will wait and start pushing when he comes."

She could not believe her eyes. The clock was ticking. After twenty minutes of waiting, she asked if I had any family member whom they could call to be with me since this was a life and death situation. Remember, I refused any pain medication this time again. I'd said, "I will go through all the pain."

I was in so much pain, and the baby wanted to come out. I could feel it in my abdomen. I raised my head and continued making *dua.* I looked at the clock and said, "He should be done and, on his way, now."

They said, "Okay, well, we are tired of waiting. You have to start pushing now." They checked the monitor and baby's heart rate had dropped a little. Now, I had to push no matter what.

I said, "Yaa Allah! I tried. Please bring my husband here quickly." I took a deep breath and screamed, "*Laa ilaaha illaAllah*" when I heard my husband panting in the hallway.

"Where is she?" Sabtiu was asking. The nurses rushed him to the delivery room, and immediately when he walked in, I gave my first full push. I was asked to take a deep breath and try again when the contractions come.

Sabtiu was in all white. I started thinking, *What if I die in this process?* I immediately started begging Allah to spare my life and the baby's life. I looked at my husband, the midwife and the two nurses who were on my sides and the room and said, "This is it."

Another contraction came, and I pushed through. It was hard that I thought I could not. I shouted, "I can't! I *can't!*"

My midwife said, "You can. You have done this before."

All I could hear was "Push, push, push, push."

Alhamdulillah, I gave it my all, and baby was here. My husband was so happy. He was shouting "*Allahu Akbar! Laa ilaaha illaAllah!*"

Sabtiu held our baby and called the *azan*, and baby was passed to me to bond with. Sabtiu cut the umbilical cord, and after I settled in and was cleaned by the nurses, he was busy making phone calls and sharing the good news with everyone.

Sabtiu called my mom first, then Ustaz Adel and then Farhya. *Alhamdulillah*, my phone was blowing up. I put it away and bonded with my bundle of joy. It was such a life changing moment.

All the pain meant nothing once I saw that beautiful "mini me." *Allahu Akbar!* Everything was worth it. *Alhamdulillah.*

40

Reaching Out for Help

When you need help, seek it. I remember in 2019, I went for therapy. Yes, THERAPY! This was a tough time for me. Our home had become a social center where different abused and frustrated Muslims were housed. I had multiple domestic violence victims staying with us, and with time, I realized that I started questioning my marriage.

I was hearing all these bad things from sisters about their husbands that it made me subconsciously start to question my marriage. *What if my husband does the same thing to me?* I had these families come in with their children, which affected my children. My children had a simple lifestyle. These kids came with gadgets and devices that were foreign to my home, and my children started gravitating towards that. It was as though I was losing the structure of my home right before my eyes. I was not happy.

I brought it up with my husband and suggested therapy. Of course, you know the response. *An African man going for therapy? No!* "I don't need anyone telling me what to do," he said. "There is nothing wrong with me." Obvious, right?

I said, "I know that, but I think we need it." I was dealing with some teenagers and their drama as well. There was a teenager who got pregnant outside of marriage. Her community abandoned her. I intervened. It was a lot, and it was causing a lot of doubts and questions in my head about love, marriage, and trust.

I realized I had to go for therapy for myself. I had been counseling the youth for years now. However, I figured I was so involved in their issues that it was affecting me a lot. I told my husband, "I will be going for therapy because I need it." He was hesitant, but I insisted, "I need it before I lose my mind."

He said, "Okay."

I made the appointment with the therapist. I remember when the day arrived my husband was being sarcastic while I was getting ready to leave. He said, "You advise people and now you need therapy? What for?"

I said, "Yes, now I need someone to help me with all of the people's problems that are in my head. Who advises the adviser?"

The first appointment was nerve wracking. Once I walked in and saw that the therapist was a young woman like me, I was kind of disappointed. I was like, *Imagine someone like me giving me advice.* I didn't want to open up. I thought this would be the first and the last appointment. *Maybe my husband was right. I don't need this. I can figure it out.*

It was as if she sensed my hesitation. She started by thanking me for coming and assuring me that there was no shame in being here and discussing the stigma associated with getting help. That eased my anxiety.

She then walked me through some basic start-up questions about my life and where I'm at. *Boy oh boy!* That was when I realized I had a lot to say. I talked and talked, and I choked. It was as if I was vomiting all that I had kept inside.

We scheduled a follow-up, and soon we became so comfortable with each other. I was advised to save and protect my home before saving others. I was doing so much that I was losing myself. I kept giving and giving and didn't have time to take care of myself. I needed some time to unwind.

I was a perfectionist. I knew that. That was not a surprise. What surprised me was when she said, "You are an Over Achiever. Some people call it High Achiever. This kind of people are never satisfied with where they are at. They always have to be doing something."

I knew that about myself, but I didn't know how deep it was. I would have ten things on my "to do" list, and once I accomplished them, I wanted more. Instead of commending myself for a job well done, I'd speak down to myself and say, *You could have done more.* I was never satisfied with my achievements. I was constantly learning, studying, and stretching myself thin. I couldn't just relax and sit and do nothing. I was not taking care of myself like I thought I was.

After five therapy sessions, I figured my mindset was linked to my upbringing. I was expected to be the best and second place was not good enough. This had followed me into adulthood, so I was in constant competition with myself.

I remember the therapist saying, "Take thirty minutes a day to just sit and relax."

I quickly said, "But I'm wasting time."

She said, "You are gaining yourself and rejuvenating so you can do more."

That truth hit me like never before. For me, I had to always be doing something fruitful. I realized I was my biggest critic. I had to quickly make some changes.

My therapist asked me, "What would happen if you fall down today and get hospitalized? What would happen to your children? What would happen to the husband whom you love dearly? You need to save 'you' before changing the world," she said. "I know you want to help everyone and fix everyone's issues but know that you have done enough. Now, we need to get you to a healthy place. You need to focus on your health and sanity for once."

That got to me. I had grown up seeing my mom do everything on point. She was a "super woman." She kept everything under control at home. *I am her daughter, so I need to do way better than she did*, I'd tell myself. Daily, I was in competition with myself but never counted my achievements. I was busy accomplishing so much that I did not bother to pause and give myself a pat on the shoulder for what I'd achieved. To hear from someone else that I needed to take care of myself was relieving and a wake-up call. I never regretted attending those sessions.

I can still be the best and take breaks, I told myself. *I can still be the best wife and mom without overworking myself. I can still be the best to everyone around me without always working and stressing out.* I had to accept this, and this was life-changing, *alhamdulillah.*

Just think about where I would have been without reaching out for help. Imagine, I stayed and never voiced what I was thinking or the doubts that had started creeping inside of me? Imagine letting all these people come in and take over my home? What would it have done to my children and us, long term?

I am grateful for getting the push and listening to my intuition that I needed therapy. I am also thankful that I was given the opportunity to get the help I needed. Not everyone has that. I know there is a stigma in the African community against therapy, but please, seek out for help if you need it. There is no shame in it. My advice is this: *Just focus on that one person, group or organization that can help you unwind your unspoken struggles and deal with them. Don't run away from your issues like most people do. Your problems will just meet you again later on in life. Deal with them now, no matter how scary the first step is!*

41

My Third Pregnancy

My third pregnancy was one that threw me off the grid. I had a lot of morning sickness, threw up at least eight times a day in the beginning. After nine weeks, it got to about nine to twelve times a day. I was so weak that I could not do anything. Then the coronavirus hit America, and then the kids had to stay indoors with us (due to social distancing from everyone else) from March 13th, 2020. *Oh boy!*

Being indoors with two boys, all day over several weeks was exhausting and exacerbating. There were days when I asked myself if I could continue with the pregnancy. This was something my husband hated to hear. Of course, he wasn't carrying the pregnancy, so it was easy for him to get mad when I made statements like that. But when you are in my situation where you throw up even the water you drink, then you might understand.

I had no energy at all to do anything. I had an unending cold, backache, headache everyday with hot flashes, and no appetite at all. I was restless because I did not know what sleeping position was the best for me.

I was used to having things in place, having a schedule and being on top of my game all the time. So, to be in a position where I was helpless, nauseated all day and stamina-less was really daunting for me. It was a nightmare, and a phase I do not ever want to be in again.

I instantly told myself, *This will be the last pregnancy.* The pregnancy came with so many difficulties that I was in the hospital at least once every week. I took different tests to just figure out what was going on.

At one point, the nurse said I might have to go into labor for the fetus to be taken out. I was like, "Oh no! That will never happen." It got to a point where I was in so much pain that I wondered if I could continue. My body gave up fighting. I could not fight anymore.

Children are a gift from God, and I love them to death, but I was not sure if I could go through this again. I did not know if I could make it through this one. *May Allah ease the burden of all pregnant women all over the world.*

My sincere advice to readers is this: *Just pray for a pregnant woman when you see her and try to help her in whatever way you can. You never know what that woman is going through. Not all of us have easy pregnancies. Some go through a STORM. When you are pregnant and you are around people who can help you, please let them help you out. It is not easy. If you can get someone to cook for you, do not hesitate.*

I am that person who does not want to bother people. However, my third pregnancy showed me that you need others on board, especially if you cannot handle it sometimes. Life is not as easy for all of us. Someone might be going through their darkness while you are going through your light. So be careful how you treat people in life.

With Hyperemesis Gravidarum (HG), my difficult pregnancies only escalated with the latter being worse than the former. My third pregnancy was the hardest pregnancy thus far. Not only was I throwing up every day since I found out that I was pregnant, but I also had been spitting and couldn't swallow saliva as much. My mouth was always bitter. My feet would get hot in the middle of the day and would be on fire in the middle of the night. I'd have heart burns and headaches almost every day. I'd suffered with an extreme cold as well even before finding out that I was pregnant. Pregnancy only escalated it.

In short, let me give you a gist of my pregnancy daily life. I wake up with headache and a cold while feeling nauseated as well. When I throw up, I throw up through my nose, mouth, and eyes. Sometimes there are traces of blood when there is nothing left in my stomach. After throwing up, I deal with a constant flow of saliva which I cannot swallow but must bring out. My feet are hot, and I have pains in my back and body. I am generally restless, and I have no appetite. I eat because I have to, so I eat whatever is available. All the way through my eating, I am thinking about throwing up afterwards. *How then does one enjoy this kind of meal?*

However, during this difficult time, my amazing boys were there to help. They gave me hugs and kisses. When things got tough and I needed a massage, they tried to give me a massage with their tiny hands. They would tell me how nice I look when I dressed up and gave me endless praises throughout the day.

My sons were a handful but, God knows I got through this pregnancy with their support. If I did not have them, I don't know what would have happened to me with all the emotional struggles I was going through. I did not enjoy this pregnancy at all because of all the symptoms I had. However, their kind gestures and love for their unborn sibling kept me going. They gave my belly kisses and cuddled me at night.

My younger son was very affectionate and creative. He made it a ritual to always kiss my belly and give me a hug every single day. He will say, "Mommy, you look beautiful." I would smile at him even though I was not feeling beautiful. He also came up with so many games we could play together.

May Allah bless them and make them treat their wives even better in the future. I am so proud of them. Today, I look at them and I say, *Alhamdulillah, I brought you up well.*

During this difficult time, I was blamed by their father for every mess they made. Every pencil that was broken in the house was my fault. Every remote that stopped working was because I allowed the kids to touch it. Every item that was put in the wrong place by the kids was my fault.

I think Sabtiu was forgetting that we had been in quarantine for almost four months by then, with two active kids who were learning and exploring daily. Meanwhile, they were flourishing and thriving in their academics and social skills.

I made sure Qur'an was read every day in the house. They learned about Islam plus fulfilled their schoolwork. *Oh, I forgot!* I'd make breakfast, lunch, and dinner daily for them and their dad. And because my condition would worsen when I cooked, the midwife suggested that I should get someone to cook for me. *But who am I to tell my African husband that I need someone to do the cooking for me?*

Sometimes, I would cough and pee at the same time. Anytime I coughed, urine came out. So, imagine how many times I'd have to redo my *wudhoo'* and change my undergarments? *It is very sad that men do not think past a lot of things in this emotional journey, especially African men.*

What woman on earth *wants* to be helpless? There were so many days when I cried and just wished that I wasn't pregnant. Don't get me wrong, babies are a blessing, and I love them. However, the difficult journey of pregnancy with its emotional struggles makes you think like that.

There were days I just sat helpless when the kids were taking a break from a lesson, and all I could do was weep. They give me a hug and say, "Mommy, you look sad." I would say, "Yes, I am sad. I am really sad because I miss my mom."

Pregnancy is a time when you need only positive vibes around you. You need unending support and encouragement. You need positive affirmations. You need help and support in house activities and chores. You need emotional and spiritual support. You need compliments because you don't even feel beautiful most of the time. You need that constant reminder. You need a massage and a back rub. You need empathy, compassion, and words of encouragement consistently and continuously.

But what do most women get? It's a time when a man shows his ugly side and cares less about his wife. Some men avoid their wives completely because they don't find them beautiful anymore. Some men start flirting outside and checking other women out. I wonder, *Do they think about how their poor wives feel? Do you know how it hurts to be betrayed especially during a time when you are helpless and need the most help possible?* I have heard a lot of horrifying stories from sisters.

Do you know how it feels to feel down constantly, and the person you think is your partner is the one that makes you feel worse in those trying times? It is painful and heartbreaking, and I hope and pray that our men, African men especially, will start to step up when their wives are pregnant. It is an uneasy time for any woman.

Some women have it easier than others, and some of us have it excruciatingly difficult. Some women have few to no symptoms at all while some of us have extreme symptoms. Some women can be pregnant and work and remain generally active. Some of us cannot work while pregnant. Some of us can also be pregnant and take care of kids while others cannot even take a shower by themselves. They need help to even do basic daily stuff.

It is sad, and it is tough. But most African men push their wives away to her family for help, so they really do not know how to handle this period or deal with it in a mature way. It is very sad, and most women dislike their men for that.

So, my advice to women out there is this: *Get all the help you can possibly get. If you have people to do dishes for you, let them do it. Even if it is someone doing your hair, let them do it for you. Don't hesitate to ask for help. Some of us are not used to asking for help, so it worsens our plight.* I pray that The Creator, Allah, eases this priceless journey for every woman.

For remember, when a woman dies during this journey, she is seen as a martyr, with direct entry into Jannah. That should tell you the extreme weight and respect that The Lord of the Worlds accords to pregnant women.

'Ubaadah ibn al-Saamit narrated that the Messenger of Allah (peace and blessings of Allah be upon him) said, "Who is counted as a *shaheed* (martyr) among you?" They said, "The one who fights and is killed for the sake of Allah." The Messenger (peace and blessings of Allah be upon him) said: "Then the martyrs among my ummah would be few. The one who is killed for the sake of Allah is a *shaheed*; the one who dies of plague is a *shaheed*; the one who dies of a stomach disease is a *shaheed*; the woman who dies with a child in her womb is a *shaheed*" (Ahmad, 5/315 and Ibn Maajah, *saheeh* by Ibn Hibbaan).

42

PARENTING

Just when you thought pregnancy was tough, you are welcomed by another period called *parenting.* I wish there was an easy recipe for parenting. *Don't we all? SubhanaAllah!* Parenting is the hardest job on the planet. This is largely because you really want to do a good job, so you keep trying, and sometimes the outcome does not match the effort that was put into it.

Here's what I tell myself: First of all, I want you to see parenting as an act of worship. Once you view it like that, it changes everything. You know it is not going to be a walk in the park. *'Ebaadah* (worship) is difficult; it requires hard work and consistency. There will be lows and highs, but we definitely want the highs to be more than the lows.

I'll share with you a few of my parenting struggles. I learned from my children that they reflect us and the environment around them.

Allah tested me by taking away the speech of my oldest son when he was two years old. My son would talk and say lots of things from when he was fourteen months old. After his eighteen months vaccination, things took a different turn.

First of all, my husband's friend was playing ignorantly with my son on the stairs in front of our apartment after our dentist appointment. He left my son alone to walk down the stairs, and he fell off and rolled down the stairs. My son bumped his mouth, and blood gushed all over the floor. My son's lips were deformed. I was so scared and worried. I called my husband right away, and as expected, he said it would go away. He didn't seem worried as I was.

I immediately entered the house and cleaned his lips and massaged them with hot water. I was thinking about taking him to the hospital. He had a fever, so I gave him Tylenol. After an hour, he seemed okay, so I fed him some food. He was able to chew, and all his teeth were intact. He was not saying anything but crying intermittently. We thought that was normal.

Several days went by, and he would not speak or say much. He started pointing a lot, and when prompted, he would just say the bare minimum. I was worried and wanted my son to be checked by the doctor, but my husband thought it was no big deal. He said, "Our son will be fine." Very typical of African men, right? He thought I was overthinking and overreacting.

I went online and read a lot of articles from Medline and BabyCenter, and it did not seem to be a big deal. The answers I got assured me that he would be fine since no tooth was broken or damaged. He just had a big sore on his lips which I treated. His words after that just took a turn for the worse.

I started questioning the vaccination. Was it the fall? Everything was happening gradually. He'd taken his eighteen-month vaccines and then went to the dentist office a few weeks afterwards before he fell off the stairs. *What is going on?* At the time, I was pregnant with his younger brother.

Some African women said, "He's just being jealous. Boys are like that. You should not worry much."

However, as a mother, I felt guilty and wanted the best for my son. I continued to read with him and read Qur'an every day. He would listen and hum along.

I later gave birth to his brother. Things took a quick turn for the worse, and he was not speaking anymore, not a word. I was so scared. People would come to visit, and he would just start crying and run away. I started worrying a lot. This was not my happy son who used to love people. What was going on? I turned to a sister who worked at a day care and had much experience with kids. She said, "Don't worry. It's just a phase."

I took him for his two-year doctor's appointment, and I brought up concerns of his speech. My doctor said I should not worry.

I started reading a lot about autism. My son would look away and not speak. All the seminars and workshops I took about developmental delays and concerns started popping into my head. But the question I asked myself was, *He was fine before, so what happened?* His dad would shun it whenever I wanted to intervene and ask for external help. Sabtiu said, "He'll be fine." Everyone said he will be fine, but I was not convinced.

His doctor said, "You should put him in a day care, and once he is around other children, he will be fine."

By then, I had been homeschooling him for two years now, and they wanted me to take him to a different setting? I thought I should give it a try. You would think things would be easy. I was blamed, and I was questioned. I decided to send him to preschool.

My son had never been with anyone else for that long. He did not drink nor eat at school. He hated it, and I disliked it. He would not look at them, and he would look away. His teachers will ask me if he smiles or speaks. My happy son was no more. I was seeing a lot of awful changes.

Was it because I had another child? Is he feeling left out? I had so many questions. My son would run to the door and play with the doorknob and keys a lot. He would rock his head a lot in the chair. He would act hyper while watching TV by jumping continuously.

I had read a lot of books about parenting and child development. All those books were haunting me now. I had so much guilt. I knew my son did not want to be in the school setting. He loved being with his mom. He would run to me whenever I came to pick him up.

Am I doing the right thing by sending him to school? Whenever I got there to pick him up, I would just be welcomed with lots of complaints. "He did not eat." "He did not even drink water." "He wants to play by himself." "He doesn't like playing with the other kids." As I stood there listening to his teachers, he would run to me and tug on me impatiently. It was clear that my son hated being there.

Am I doing the right thing for him? Is he making any progress? But I am just following the doctor's advice. To add insult to injury, his lead teacher told me, "Start learning sign language because he might not talk again, so you might need it."

He is just two years two months old now, I thought. *Why is everyone making it hard for me?* I had to take matters into my own hands. I made an urgent appointment with his doctor and wrote exactly what my concerns were. I told her what I thought and that I was worried he might be autistic.

She said, "He is not autistic."

I told her some of the things I'd read about autism. She checked him out and ruled out the diagnosis. I was relieved. *So now, what was the matter?*

I informed her that things went downhill after his eighteen-month vaccination. Afraid of the consequences, she squashed that argument quickly and said, "He will catch up in preschool." She assured me, "He has been the only child for all these years, and that is why he is acting like that." I requested an official evaluation because I was not satisfied.

She gave me contacts of a social worker, and I had to call to make the appointment to get a referral for an evaluation. I did, but the social worker was out of office. After daily calls and leaving voice messages, the social worker got back to me and gave me a list of phone numbers of agencies to call and get the evaluation done. I made a series of phone calls and was turned down by some while others referred me to several others as well.

After a week of intensive daily phone calls and explaining my son's situation, I finally landed a deal with CityPro Group. You would think it would be easy. *No!* I had to come to their office and do a lot of paperwork. Mind you, I had a newborn who was also just two months old then.

Winter had started, and I would go with him in the cold from office to office. You cannot imagine how many offices and meetings at different locations I visited just to set the ball rolling. I wanted the evaluation immediately, so I could not wait. I had to work extra hard.

I basically did everything on my own and on December 27th, the first evaluation happened, *alhamdulillah.* However, even this evaluation got canceled earlier because I did not have an interpreter. Apparently, it is part of the process.

I made it clear that there was no way I would get a Kotokoli interpreter for my son. We finally got a Hausa interpreter who could speak some Kotokoli to come on December 27th. The evaluation finally happened, and lo and behold, my son was approved for speech services, for speech therapy. I was so excited about it.

But how soon? They explained that it would take about two weeks for her to write the report from the evaluation, and I would have to sign some agreements and then receive some phone calls from speech therapists to set up the date and times with me. I asked her, "Do you need help to speed it up? I can help you out"

She laughed and said, "You are an amazing mom! You are doing a good job. I have not seen any mother in your condition doing this much." I was breastfeeding my newborn and typing with the other hand on my phone, recording some of the observations I had during the evaluation. This was because I did not want to forget and also because I wanted to make her work easier.

I told her I was available to type if she needs me. I had to turn in some paperwork which I could fax to expedite, so I did. *Alhamdulillah*, my son started speech therapy in January. By this time, he was already reading Qur'an daily and was in Suratu Duha with a few mispronunciations here and there. He could read all the Arabic alphabets and Arabic numbers. Teaching him Qur'an was easy, so I had hope that my son would speak again.

43

Raising My Older Son

One morning as I was worried because he refused every breakfast I gave him before leaving for school. I ran to the bedroom and started crying while breastfeeding his younger brother. I looked up toward the sky and asked Allah for help. I said, "O Allah! You know I have done everything possible to help him. Now I leave it in Your hands. He spoke before, and now You have taken his speech away. Please send it back, and I will be grateful."

I'd just finished saying this dua when I heard my son shout from the living room, "Sweet potato pie!" His dad was sitting in confusion looking at him.

Holding my baby on my chest, I ran to the living room. I asked his dad, "Did I hear him right?"

Sabtiu smiled happily and said, "I told you he would speak." *Wallahi*, it was this day that changed everything. Now, I was convinced my son would speak. It was just a matter of time.

I told my son, "Don't worry. We will get you sweet potato pie after school, *inshaaAllah*." I did as I promised, and he enjoyed it.

My son was still not eating at school. He would stay hungry from the morning when we dropped him until 2:00 p.m. when I came to pick him up. He would always run to me, and I would tell myself, *Once my son gets the social skills he needs, he'll be out of here.*

I knew my son did not like being at the school. As we walked to catch the bus home, he would smile at me and look happy holding my hands. His baby brother would be in the baby carrier on my chest. There would be times when they would both be crying, and I would have to get to a spot to calm them down. Sometimes I was holding both of them on my laps at the same time. I had my nursing cover everywhere I went. I would breastfeed on the train, in the bus and in the taxi depending on our mode of transportation.

There would be days that the bus would not show up, and we would wait for a taxi in the rain or in the snow, but the joy and warmth of my smile was enough for my kids. There were days when I looked so helpless, and my son would wipe my tears at the bus stop with his small hands. Sometimes people would look at me pitifully as I tried to stop the bus so I could go to the nearest restroom or any available restaurant to change my baby's diaper and breastfeed him. I could not stand in the bus and breastfeed while the bus was full and there was no spot to sit.

I knew all of this would pay off one day. Our routine was to say our *duas* once we got home. My son would not respond but would always hum along and look happily to me. He would get his speech therapy twice each week for thirty minutes. I would watch closely as his therapist did her job.

His speech therapist would mostly be at our house for twenty-five minutes, relax for five minutes and would be gone. I would then give my son a thirty-minute break, and then we would recite Qur'an. Everyday, we had to recite Qur'an. Once I recited Qur'an with him for over 30 minutes, I would then give him 30 minutes of TV to watch an Islamic show while I recited Qur'an to his baby brother.

After that, I would start making dinner. As I made dinner, I would play with them intermittently. The TV was off after thirty minutes for play time. In between making dinner and playing with them, we would pause for Asr and make *wudhoo'* together. I made sure baby was close by watching us. After Asr prayer, we would review our Arabic alphabets, Arabic numbers, and months in Islam. Then we had *nasheed* time where I would sing some Islamic songs with them and a few nursery rhymes from school. I would then organize and fix the house before Daddy came home. It was a routine of a stay-at-home mom, or what most people call a housewife. I loved it, but it was very time-consuming.

At the time, my husband was getting an additional degree, and I had to help with his assignments and projects while making sure he met all his deadlines for class. I was dealing with teaching my son after school and caring for a newborn, forgetting myself at this point. I hardly had time to take care of myself like I should have done. I did not get the necessary time to heal.

Where was the time? I had to wake up early and get my older son ready for school or the masjid on the weekends. Not forgetting, I went back to teaching after three and a half months of maternity break at the Weekend Islamic School.

However, people who did not know my story would see me and just think I am lazy. The common misconception of stay-at-home mothers is that they are just lazy and eating and sleeping all day. I wish it was that easy. Well, maybe for some people that is the case. However, I can assure you that I have met several homemakers who are excelling at various ventures.

Back to my son's struggle-this continued for a while, and I gradually started seeing progress. His therapist loved me because we worked as a team. She answered my concerns and questions. Sometimes, she herself could not show up because she had her own family issues to deal with, but I had her back. I quickly learned from her and became a substitute for her when she was unable to be there. *Her work is not that difficult*, I thought. However, it took skill and real patience to do this. I thought of exploring that career, but I realized that my son needed me full time.

I created a vision board and set the pace for what he would be accomplishing in the next three months. I would go online and read some parenting tips from the parenting resource hub that I had learned about from previous seminars and workshops. I was also taking classes at night when they were asleep. I was pursuing a Certificate in Education.

Almost every seminar and workshop that I learned about, I attended. I left no stone unturned. Before long, my son was speaking in full sentences and a few compound sentences, *alhamdulillah*. By the time he was three, he was speaking okay. *Alhamdulillah*. There were still some struggles here and there, but I was there to guide him through. This testing time was full of battles, and the people around us did not help much.

Fortunately, when it came to Qur'an, there were no mistakes in his recitation, and by the age of three, he had completed half of Juz 'Amma (the last thirtieth of the Qur'an), *alhamdulillah*.

I remember crying in silence when we came from our weekend classes sometimes. Socially, my son was worse at the masjid because he was so often in the spotlight. Everyone wanted to hold him, pick him up, talk to him, or teach him something. They meant well; however, the outcome was not always good.

Also, I realized my son was picking up a lot of bad behaviors. He was getting frustrated a lot at the masjid. He began hitting, and it was getting bad. Anytime someone asked him to stop, he would hit more. The kids at the masjid would then shout at him and shame him when he did that. I would try to take him out of the situation for the most part.

Farhya was the only one who was patient with this behavior. It was tough on me. I wanted my son to act his best, but his worst came out in the house of Allah. *Why is that?* I started thinking about it. *SubhanaAllah!* I realized he saw the teachers at the masjid hitting kids when they didn't listen. That was how they got them to listen. Hence, that was his way of getting what he wanted as well.

I spoke with my husband about it and of course, as can be expected, he shunned it instantly. However, I was looking at the bigger picture, my son's observation. He was very attentive, taking in all that he saw and learning a lot even though he did not say much. I realized the influence an atmosphere can have on a child. I realized if I could not change the environment, I could help my son's coping mechanism.

I spoke with Farhya and explained what was going on in my son's head, and she understood. She would mostly come to his rescue in my absence or when I was engaged with some other student. The others did not get it. They either said demeaning words about my son or shook their heads in amusement or just ignored him and gave him nasty looks.

I felt hurt as a mother. They did not understand that he was trying hard to make sense of everything around him.

At school, he was beginning to get comfortable, and the teachers were becoming more understanding there. The assistant teacher who used to rain me with insults for homeschooling my son started liking me more now. I had taken all her insults and blame with a smile. There were so many moments I wanted to talk back, but I stopped myself.

Now, he was the star of the class. He was the lead poem reciter in his Stepping Up ceremony. My patience had paid off. Today, I look at my son and think, *What a journey!* I went through all of this by myself for the most part. Almost everyone second guessed me, thought I was worrying too much or stressing myself. I asked myself, *What would I do if my son grows up and asks me, "Why didn't you do this or that for me?" Above all, what would I tell Allah?*

That was my motivation for all the meetings, for all the follow ups, for all the reciting Qur'an on the train, and saying the *Salawat* (sending prayers of peace and blessings) upon the Prophet Muhammad, *sallallaahu'alayhi wa sallam*, every Friday whether we were indoors or outdoors. Everything was strategic. Everything was intentional. I was looking at the bigger picture, and I had my vision board to check off and revise items as we went.

Dear reader, I share with you these intimate and private encounters so you can take a lesson. I struggled with my son, but I knew I did not want to be a "good" mother. I wanted to be an exceptional and outstanding mother. I had no model to look at in my unique case, but I would visit the stories in the Qur'an from time to time. I would wonder how the mother of Mariam (Mary) was able to say the dua she said, and how Mariam the mother of Jesus (peace be upon them) turned out the way she did. What about the story of Luqman and his son? And the story of Ibrahim (Abraham) and his sons Ishmael and Ishaq (Isaac)? Our situations were different, but there were gems I could learn from.

There were days I would cry non-stop wishing my mom was close by to help me. I knew I had no mom or dad to turn to here in New York, but I had memories of my childhood to look back on. I had memories of growing up in Nima. I had memories of surviving in a tough neighborhood. I took the good from my childhood and implemented them into my parenting. As for the "not good" part, I promised myself not to repeat it. This is difficult because occasionally, I do lose it and yell here and there, but I quickly realize it and apologize to my children. I figured that my children would come out the way I treated them. When I wrong them, I apologize. I do not say, *I am the mom, and they are the children, so I am not going to apologize.*

As Africans, that is how most of us grew up. No adult apologizes to you; you are the child, and they are the adult. Adults were never wrong. I knew how hurt that made me feel growing up. I did not want my children to feel that way, so I accepted my errors and mistakes and apologized. I cheered my children on when they did amazing and was there every step of the way.

Sabtiu helped when he could. Remember, he worked hard to provide for us. I also made sure the home was conducive and comfortable for all. My mom was an outstanding mom. She was always on the same page with my dad. There was no way you could let her go against my dad, so I made sure my husband and I were on the same page as much as I could. Even if we were not, I did not make it visible to the kids. The home was always loving and flourishing. My children were always learning, even when we were having fun.

44

The Blessing of Sisterhood

I have met some amazing sisters in my life. I can only speak of the ones I met since marrying and moving to New York City. I have come across a lot of sisters and mothers through teaching and counseling the youth at the masjid. However, three of them stand out.

Farhya is like my younger sister. I call her my sister even though we are not from the same mother, and we are not related in anyway, except through Islam. I heard about Farhya before moving to America. My husband told me about the students at his madrasa and she stood out. He said she was well behaved and respectful.

I came to the masjid, and when I met her, it was exactly as I heard about her. She was all smiles in her crutches at the time because she'd broken her leg. I said salaam to her, and we exchanged a lot of smiles without saying much. I was teaching the children's class then, but she would leave the teenagers' class and come to my class occasionally.

Eventually, she stopped attending her class and made my class her class. I was worried, but after speaking with her *Ustaz*, he said it was okay. We became friends since. Till today, the dynamic of our relationship is very interesting. It is organic and effortless. I know when to be her teacher, friend, and sister. When I am teaching, I am her teacher, and she has no special treatments.

During counseling period after class, I am her friend. When she visits me at home and we hang out, I am her sister. We have been through a lot together. A book is not enough to talk about her. Through the ups and downs and the betrayals in the student body and community, she has been with me through it all. I hope I am the same for her.

I remember when my son and husband were in a fatal car accident in 2018. It was as if my world had crumbled. I was so scared and fearful. A hit-and-run had taken place. My husband was unconscious with blood on his face and my son was speechless. They were dragged in the ambulance with blood all over my husband. My legs were shaking and could not carry me.

I had my younger son at home, so I could not follow them in the ambulance. I was shaking and unable to speak. I gathered myself and left a voice note for her since she was in Africa then. She quickly called and consoled me. There were others there who eventually heard it and called to check on us.

I really hated it when people asked about the car. My concern was my husband and son. I would give a zillion cars away to have my husband and son intact like nothing happened. Some people would call and ask about them in seconds and quickly focus on the car. They would ask, "Did you have insurance?" "Would you be getting a new car?" *Who cares about a piece of metal? I am worried about their lives while some people were worried about the material items.*

Farhya was one of the few who consoled me for days and checked on me for three days straight. Those were three of the most difficult days of my life. I was numb, and I could not eat. I was only drinking water. It was a deep shock. Just seeing my beloved husband and son back home safely from the emergency room was a blessing. I was asked to observe my son and bring him back if anything was off. I was like a satellite on both of them. I was watching and taking note of their actions wherever they went. Farhya was there for me even though she was a thousand miles away.

For all my children's naming ceremonies, she helped cooked the food for the crowd. It was in New York City, and you would think people would come around to help you out. However, everyone was busy with their lives. Farhya was there to bring me food just days after I had my second child. She was there babysitting my boys so my husband could be with me in the labor ward while I gave birth to my daughter.

Farhya was there when I needed someone to look after the kids so I could hang out with my husband. She was there to go with me for appointments that required another person when my husband was not available. My kids love her, and she loves them. She has been my rock during my maternal break from the masjid. When there was heresy in the community, she stood by us and never betrayed us like most people did.

When I decided to write a book, Farhya was among the few I told. She was so excited and asked to help with resources to make it happen. My mother loves her even though she has not met her. My kids love her so much, and I love her. She is my tribe.

Here's my advice to my sisters: *Find that one sister or sisters that bring the best in you and mingle with them. Life is too short. Take out the negativity and stay away from the gossip and backbiting. Stay away from the people who do not make you better. Find your tribe. That person does not have to be from your country or speak your native language. Once the person fears Allah and brings out the best in you, they are your tribe. Find that tribe and hold onto it in truth. May Allah grant us all our tribe.*

My second sister is Ferouz. She is another student I met but was not close to initially. She was not regular to class. She was working on the weekends and came on her days off. She was quiet. Later, her dad arranged for her to be coming home to learn with me after I had my first child.

She would frequently visit and learn. Sometimes she would stay just for 15 minutes and leave. With time, she improved, and we could do thirty minutes at a time. We gradually became close as sisters and friends. Ferouz was the first female to visit me at the hospital when I had my second child. I was craving for some pizza, and she got that for me.

The parents of Ferouz and her sister, Hansah, are all beloved to me. I love the entire family. They are so respectful and genuine. Unlike some families who smile at you and talk bad about you behind your back, this family is genuine. They remind their kids to be respectful, and even the parents are more respectful, *Allahu Akbar!* They would call to thank us and visit us from time to time to see the progress of their children. *Alhamdulillah*, both daughters have completed the recitation of the Qur'an with my little support.

Ferouz has been there just like Farhya has been. There are times that I am torn regarding who among these two I like the best. I love them both the best. Ferouz has helped me through several evaluations for my son. She has been there to babysit my children so I could go for my doctor's appointment too. She always knew my cravings during my pregnancies and got them for me when she came to visit.

You would think she would stop visiting after she was done reciting the entire Qur'an. Nope! She still visits, calls, and checks on us. We have traveled together several times, and her composure and character even in the worst scenarios were mind boggling.

My final special sister is Ummu Bilal, an exceptional sister. I met her when we formed a mother's support group for our community. We called it Muslim Parents Circle (MPC), and I am one of the key members.

The first time I met Ummu Bilal in person was exceptional. She was coming to New York City for our meeting, all the way from New Jersey. She met the group with smiles and was focused on me as I was speaking when she walked in. She said salaam, sat and joined the group. She was late. However, once I was done, she immediately said, "You must be Mariam. The way you speak and the way you type in the group are the same." I smiled and hugged her instantly. Our children were there. I connected with Hamza, her second son, right away.

Her oldest son has autism. She has gone through a lot with him. I eventually met him at subsequent meetings. We got along just right. As other sisters were looking at him weird and wondering why he acted the way he did, I smiled and came around. I was intrigued by his world. He saw things differently. He was very smart. He said things people did not understand, but I did. Ummu Bilal was so gentle and understanding. It was as though I saw a sister who saw parenting like I did, a nurturing gentle journey. She was honest and loving. Her smiles and hugs were always warm.

She is a sister I loved from day one, and my love for her has not changed since. She has shown me that no matter how your child is, be proud of them! She had dealt with many issues with her children and family that when you hear about them, you cannot help but cry. We have become so close since.

The other sisters cannot help but gush over our sisterhood, *alhamdulillah*. Ummu Bilal is down to earth and very willing to learn. She is one sister that admires every other sister's journey. She has words of encouragement. When people would blame us, the *Ustazs* (i.e., the teachers), for actions done by the students at the madrasa, she would encourage me with motivational words. *May Allah bless you with a sister like this lady, Ameen.*

You do have your tribe...just look around.

May Allah bless them and make them all better than I perceive them, Allahuma Aameen.

45

Life in Lockdown

Lockdown gave us a small taste of what the last day on earth might look like. People started refocusing on what was important, the family unit. Working mothers realized how much they'd missed out in their children's lives. Full time mothers had more on their plates than ever before. Fathers had to realize how much heat their wives were going through nurturing the home. The entire globe was made to reflect and appreciate what they hadn't appreciated before.

I lost my "grandma" (a co-wife of my paternal grandmother). I lost an aunt. I lost other extended family members. I was bereaved, and I cried a lot. I made lots of *duas* and was mostly down. I was reminded of how short life was. I spoke to my "grandma" just about a week before she passed away. I spoke to my aunty a few days before she passed away. To this day, I am holding onto the conversation we had and cherishing those moments. Allah inspired me to talk to them and speak with them. I am sure, if it wasn't for the lockdown, I would not have had the chance to do that.

I had spent the past years worried and teaching other children. I had spent the last several years away from my birth family to start my own family. I had transitioned from a Nima girl to a New Yorker. Every weekend since 2014, I had been busy teaching and counselling. Suddenly, COVID-19 shut everything down. To my utter dismay, not even a text message or a phone call for over a month from these students whom I put my life on the line for.

I felt so devastated and betrayed. I felt let down. I was pregnant and emotional. I almost died. I was in a lot of pain. It was always one thing or the other when I went for my doctor's appointment. It was hard to know what was wrong with me, but I was continuously told I needed to be observed.

To make matters worse, I reached out to the other *Ustazs* and realized none of the students or parents had reached out to them as well. Our senior *Ustaz* and Director was ill and bedridden for some days. It broke my heart. It was as if I'd never taught these students anything. Where were the topics on Islamic manners that we'd discussed in class? What happened to the student-teacher relationship we'd talked about? My students were not children, they were teenagers and young adults.

These were the same students that I'd unconsciously given up my family and friends for. When I first came to New York City and started teaching at the madrasa, I would call my family on the weekend after class sometimes. Gradually, I stopped because of the workload of counseling my students after class. All my subsequent weekends, except Ramadan, were spent with these children, mostly teenagers and young adults now. And what do I get in return? I mean, I did not expect them to reward me or put me on some pedestal. No! Neither did I expect them to make me the center of their world. I just expected some concern from them.

Lockdown had hit for almost two months and none of them had reached out, except Farhya. Imagine what I went through. I was thinking, *How is it that weekends would pass by, and they do not even bother to send me a text message or call me to check on me?* These were the same teenagers that were active on Whatsapp, Facebook and Snapchat. I was really let down! That was when I knew I had to hit the *reset* button.

Those same family members and friends whose calls I'd rejected, declined, or never replied to, were the ones reaching out to me to find out if I was doing okay. They saw on the news that New York was hit dominantly by COVID-19. I had to start making calls and repairing friendships that were broken. I started apologizing and asking for forgiveness. I realized how important family was. I realized that, if I were to die today, these students would not care much. It would be my family that would be most affected. I owned my mistakes, and I shifted my life. I took all the *negative energy* out.

I remember before Ramadan 2020, I sent a voice note to my students Whatsapp group. I told them how disappointed I was in them and how I thought we were a family. Of course, you could guess what happened afterwards. There were calls here and there and text messages flooding my phone. I accepted them eventually, but I can say, I do not see these students the same way I saw them before quarantine.

It does not mean I would stop helping them. It just means I will be careful and only do what I can. I will not bring their problems to my home and wallow and consume my peace with their troubles. It means I will set boundaries on how much of my time I can share with them. It means when family reaches out, I will answer or return their calls immediately. I will gladly put my students on hold and attend to a family emergency. I have no expectations from any of them.

Moving forward, what they do will not affect me much. But you know what? I should not have expected anything in the first place. Lockdown really helped me reflect and ponder. I honor and treat them no different than I did before. The main reminder now is to not *expect anything* from them. I have never been happier.

Lockdown has helped me see my husband in a whole different light. I know how important *Jumu'ah* Salah is to him. To see him shattered, confused and desperate during Jumu'ah time in lockdown was devastating for me to watch.

The joy on the faces of my kids when I taught them during the weekend was priceless. Before lockdown, our weekends were spent at the mosque, which we loved. My kids got the leftovers when I came home. With lockdown, they had me fully to themselves and were studying the Qur'an at a rapid pace, *alhamdulilah*. They were happy to be with Mommy and Daddy all the time. They were happy to play soccer with their mom and dad indoors. They were happy to play water games and wrestle with me. It was this joy and priceless satisfaction that I remain so grateful for.

Lockdown made me reflect on my life thus far. I reflected on my childhood and my upbringing in Nima. Growing up, I wanted to become a journalist so I could tell the world about my people in the Zongo, especially Nima. I also wanted to become a doctor to cure the sick who could not afford the expensive hospital bills. I later disliked it because there was immense pressure from others that made it look like the only way to success or to prove your smartness was to become a doctor. I wanted to change the narrative, so I tossed the "Doctor dream" into the garbage. I knew I could still be an awesome person without becoming a doctor.

Then I wanted to become a lawyer; to fight for the underserved, forgotten and marginalized people in my community. I fought a lot as a child not because I was a bad child, but because I wanted to help the people who could not fight for themselves. I ended up fighting their battles. After University, my dream changed entirely to working with people in the nonprofit industry. However, after becoming a mother, I then wanted to work with children.

Now, I ended up becoming an ADVOCATE-for children, youth, and families. I get to speak and fight for people who cannot speak for themselves. I make the stories of these people heard, acknowledged, and cherished.

Nima gave me the resilience I wanted, the life lessons I needed, and the empathy to keep going. There are many talents around us. Let us not limit people based on where they come from.

Dear reader, here are my questions for you: *What are the lessons you learned from lockdown? What would you do differently? How has your life changed moving forward?* Well, I have learned a lot, and I am facing life more fully and cautiously than I ever had. I am striving each day to be the best wife, mother, sister and daughter I can be. *What are your takeaways? What do you wish to leave behind? If you were to die today, are you ready? What would you be remembered for?* I am leaving behind a letter to my children, your children, and our children at large in the *ummah.*

PART FIVE

A LETTER TO MY CHILDREN

Mu'awiyah ibn Jahima reported: Jahima came to the Prophet, peace and blessings be upon him, and he said, "O Messenger of Allah, I intend to join the expedition and I seek your counsel." The Prophet said, "Do you have a mother?" He said yes. The Prophet said, "Stay with her, for Paradise is beneath her feet."

—*Sunan al-Nasaa'I, 3104,* Sahih by Al-Albani

46

DEAR TAQWA

In the name of Allah, The Beneficent, The Merciful. I pray for peace and for blessings unto our beloved and the beloved of the Creator, Muhammad, Sallallaahu'alayhi wa sallam. I have a lot to say to you, my beloved children. May Allah protect you and preserve you and uplift you all in ranks in this world and the next.
Allahuma Ameen.

Dear Taqwa,

I have always loved the idea of having baby boys. However, it was different when I had you. *SubhanaAllah!* It was a different kind of love. It was so deep and immense. When I found out that I was pregnant with you, I prayed to Allah to bless me with a girl. Your father longed for a daughter, and I wanted to see him have his own. The way he cuddles and enjoys playing with other people's daughters was heartwarming.

This pregnancy was the most difficult one of all; not because it was a girl this time, but because you were too strong for my tummy to handle. I made lots of dua. In the early stages, I almost lost you. *SubhanaAllah!*

I was in so much pain. There were times I felt so much back pain as if I was in labor. I went for a checkup, and I was told if it continues, I will have to go to the labor ward for them to take the fetus out. The nurse was so heartless. She said this with a cold heart and no emotion. Mind you! Lockdown had just hit, and we were two weeks into COVID-19 quarantine here in New York.

I left the hospital feeling angry and had a lot of mixed emotions. *Why am I in so much pain?* My second pregnancy had been painful too, but it got better during the last trimester. *Is this going to be the same? Is it another boy?* People say carrying boys are hard and difficult. I had so many questions going through my mind.

Oh! Before that, I had gone through a lot of changes in my body. My tummy was getting big from the sides, and I was losing my breath sometimes. I'd also get tired easily. Now that I found out that I was pregnant, everything made sense. I was given asthmatic medication even though I was not asthmatic. A lot of craziness happened. It was different nurses each time I went to the hospital. Everyone had something unique to say.

The next appointment, I had an ultrasound, and I was so excited to hear I was carrying twins…or so I thought. The lady said, "It is a single baby."

I asked, "Are you sure? The pain is too much. All this pain and just one baby?" *Astaghfirullah* (may Allah forgive me). It was hard to believe. I was not able to sleep at night. I had allergies and was coughing a lot. I was sneezing as well with a bad cold. I also had itchy eyes at night with a lot of discomfort. I started breathing hard and could hardly breathe as I was lying on the bed in the ultrasound room.

The lady quickly asked for a doctor to come in. She said, "This is not normal." She asked when the difficulty of breathing started.

I said, "Around January 2020. Now, it is just getting worse."

She quickly fixed her mask tightly and added another one. She asked me to put on mine properly. I told her, "I'm finding it hard to breathe, and you expect me to cover my nose with the mask again?"

She said, "Well, we must figure out what is going on."

The doctor came in and asked a few questions. She said, "It is not COVID based on the symptoms. However, if it continues with non-stop coughing, you should rush to the emergency room."

I was so shocked. What was going on? No one could figure out what was going on with me. I thought better days were ahead. Boy oh boy! If only I'd known that the past weeks would be the best ones, I would have cherished them more. I was in for an awakening of a lifetime. The following months were a series of nightmares with the preceding less than the next. This was nothing I was prepared for.

I dressed up and put on my mask which the nurse kept insisting I wore. I was like, "Can I just get a break and wear my jilbab first?"

Alhamdulillah! It was not COVID. But I was a little sad inside. I'd forced myself to believe I was carrying twins because of the excruciating pains I was going through. I wondered, *Could she be mistaken?* Before leaving, I said, "Are you sure it is just one baby, with all these symptoms?"

She said, "Yes."

I left very disappointed. I left her office and said to myself, *Well, now I know I am carrying one baby*. The next thing that came to mind was, *Is it a boy or a girl?*

My pregnancies have always been difficult, but nothing like this. This was extreme. It was as if my lungs were being pulled out when I lay down. When I'd lie on my side, my back would hurt and when I lay on my back, my chest would hurt badly. Lying on the stomach is not Islamic, but that was the only position that gave me comfort. I felt guilty anytime I lay on my tummy, but that was the only thing that kept me going.

Night time was the worst. I was there watching your father sleep and snore. It was so hard to watch. I would get so mad sometimes that I wished I could transfer the pregnancy to him for the night.

I would wake up about six to eight times to pee. Sometimes I peed on myself before getting to the bathroom. Then, I had to change clothes again and again. Anytime I coughed, it was accompanied by some urine. I would be in *Salah* and almost done but then a cough would come and then urine would come with it, which invalidated my Salah. Now I'd have to go make a new *wudhoo'* and then try praying without coughing. This often continued for three to four times in one Salah. Salah became very difficult for me.

I started sitting to pray since it was a little better. There would be times I wanted to cough badly, but I would hold it. Imagine trying to hold a cough in Salah, it was the worst feeling ever. Also, I had this cold that never left. It would get a little better and then became worse again. Because I was pregnant, I was limited with what I could take for medication, and I could not take anything containing alcohol. Sometimes, even getting the proper medication took forever. Different nurses recommended different things.

I hated going to the doctor's office because I felt bad going but felt worse afterwards. The doctor's office was supposed to make you feel better, but it didn't. I complained, and I was told because of COVID-19 I had to see any available OB/GYN.

Did I tell you I was throwing up about eight to twelve times a day? Oh! And I was taking care of your brothers as well. Their schooling, Qur'an lessons, cooking and cleaning. Daddy started working from home later. He was getting mad at your brothers' interruption and noise making in the house. This made me feel worse. Coupled with all the emotional turmoil and physiological imbalances, I had to figure out routines and schedules to keep them busy so Daddy could work uninterrupted at home.

I could have chosen the easy way some parents choose: let them watch TV or be on their iPad, but I did not. I wanted to be the best parent for you all, so I was always conscious of that. They had thirty to sixty minutes of screen time a day. There would be days that I would be so tired and exhausted from all the routines.

I was angry at your dad. Any little chance or time he had; he left the house. In retrospect, I think he was struggling with working from home. He was not used to it. That was when I thought he would be empathetic towards me, who was going through a lot, coupled with taking care of your brothers.

Things moved from bad to worse. At this point, I had to bring it up at my next appointment. I was vomiting blood. I was not gaining weight. I threw up the little I ate. Your brothers were schooling online, and I had to cook every day, while trying to avoid the smell. The smell made me throw up or spit the more, but I had no option because there was no food to buy outside. All the restaurants were shut due to COVID-19. The only shops that were open were the grocery stores and pharmacies. It was really a tough time!

Also, I was given a wrong medication at the next appointment. I was seen by that crazy nurse who'd said I would have to go to the labor ward if the pain continued. Because of my unstable symptoms, I had to go to the hospital almost every week to be checked.

I started losing myself. At this point, I was getting mad at everything. Your brothers were my source of happiness. I would cry and they would wipe my tears. I would feel weak, and they would massage my waist, neck and back. Your brothers would quickly come and help me with their tiny hands. I was in excruciating pain.

This continued for a while. My legs would be hot and feel like they were on fire. I would keep saying, "My feet are hot and feel like they are on fire." I would keep moving and swinging them when I went to bed.

It was at eight months that I realized I could not take it anymore. One day as I was using the restroom, I reached for my favorite blue bucket, put some cold water into it and put my legs inside. This was the best feeling ever. I did not want to take my feet out. I felt so good and better. Since then, anytime the pain came, I instantly got some cold water and put my feet in it. It felt so much better, and I slept peacefully that night.

There were days when the weather would be so hot at night that even the fan could not help. I would be without clothes. I became so heavy that I needed support just to get out of bed. There would be days that I would try about five times before I could lift myself out of bed. I would throw up on myself on the way to the bathroom, which meant a change of clothes again.

There would be nights that the noise of me throwing up would wake your brothers up. They would quickly run to the bathroom like soldiers. "Oh mommy! Are you okay? You throw up too much."

I would say, "Pray for me."

They would rub my belly and tap my shoulders. "It will be okay," they would say.

Every day was like a punishment at this point, and I would go see the doctor once a week, and there would be no progress.

I was not dilating even though I was in a lot of pain. At week thirty-nine, I was still not dilated. At week forty, the midwife said, "You are almost one centimeter dilated."

The following week would be no different. There was no progress made.

With Coronavirus and everything going on in the world, I was told to go for a coronavirus test two days before my due date.

The following week on a Tuesday, I left the house with the hope of getting my test done and hopefully getting the labor nurses to check how dilated I was and be admitted. Because of last time, I was not vocal about my thoughts this time. I kept it all in my head. I must give it to your dad though. He stayed at home with your brothers so I could go for my appointments.

I got there and after waiting for a long while, the doctor's assistant put the nose swab deep down my nose, and I coughed so bad because of how intrusive and deep he went. He then said he still did not get what he wanted. After several trials, his boss came up and said, "We have to do it again."

I was like, "What? After all that discomfort?"

He said, "Unfortunately, yes."

He swabbed it, and it was not as deep as his assistant did. I was asked to come on Thursday for the result. However, if it was positive, the hospital would call me.

I asked the nurses to check how dilated I was, and they said they could not do it because I was not in pain or having contractions. Somehow, I was in pain, but it was not as bad. I insisted, "I just want to know how dilated I am." The nurses gave another excuse that I might be infected due to invasion when not needed. After going back and forth, I realized they would not do it, so I gave up and left.

It was a tough and a long walk back home. I cried, I sighed, and I got angry. "I was in a lot of pain, but nobody seemed to care," I thought. I came home disappointed but hopeful that my body might start some serious contractions in some few hours, and I would have to go back to the hospital.

My kids were disappointed. "Baby didn't come out?" they asked.

I said, "No, not yet."

That night was a nightmare. I was in tears all night and crying to my Lord to see me through. I was crying for a safe delivery. At this point, I had gone through so much that I did not know how much more I could take. I just begged Allah to see me through and I would not ask for another child after this one. I felt as though Allah was teaching me a lesson for constantly and continuously praying for a child, and then later, praying for a girl nonstop.

Wednesday was no different. Thursday came, the day I was supposed to be induced since baby wasn't here and it had been forty-two weeks already and some days. I took my shower and kissed the boys and asked for their prayers and left after Ferouz came to babysit them. Dad was at work and Ferouz had a 1:00 p.m. class as well. I told her, "Hopefully, the next call from me will be a delivery call." If only I knew what was coming.

I got to the hospital walking in my burgundy jilbab and African cloth mask. I went through security and the lady at the door taking the temperature said, "This baby should come out already. You are too tired and too big."

I said, "She is coming out today whether she likes it or not because I cannot take it anymore."

I went to the labor floor, the sixth floor. I signed in and went straight to triage. Lo and behold! They gave me a bed and told me, "It is a busy day today."

I was later informed that the attending doctor is a male, and I was so upset. I was told there was nothing that could be done. I refused to be seen by a male. I refused for a male to help me deliver the baby. I refused and I was told I would have to wait for the next day to get a midwife.

47

Baby Daughter and Postpartum

Long story short, it was Friday morning when my midwife arrived. *Alhamdulillah*, it was just her and another midwife. My husband joined in and before we knew it, our princess arrived. Sabtiu called the azan, kissed my forehead, congratulated me, and left for Jumu'ah Salah. Just as I was bonding and breastfeeding my princess, something unusual happened. I was still bleeding a lot.

My midwife was concerned. I bled a lot. It was not normal. Well, she was a very big baby, and it was a natural birth like all my births, *alhamdulillah*. This was the biggest baby I'd ever pushed. *Alhamdulillah,* I was so grateful. My midwife was still observing me and was worried. She gave me different medications to stop the bleeding. It did not stop.

She called her supervisor. She also suggested other medications, and I was injected with one that would help stop it. My baby was sent downstairs to the maternity ward nursing area for her to sleep so I could rest and join her soon.

My phone was blowing up with messages. I knew my husband had told the world by then. I quickly silenced my phone and started reminiscing on all that had happened. I was feeling so blessed and thankful. I was really hungry too. Now, I was allowed to drink some water, *alhamdulillah*. However, I could not eat because I was still being monitored.

After several hours, my midwife came in and said I might need surgery. "We will have to take your uterus or womb out," she said. "You have lost a lot of blood. This is not normal for a natural birth."

I was speechless. Everything was okay until she said this. I said, "No!"

She said, "We might have to do this to save you. We do not know what is going on. You are still bleeding."

I said, "It is normal. It will stop by itself."

She kept shaking her head. She looked worried. That worried me. Sabtiu had gone home to make some food for me.

Who can I share this news with?

I refused the operation, and she said, "You will be observed until the bleeding stops."

It reduced, but it was still coming out more than expected. I was not worried. Allah blessed me with some *emaan*, and inward, I was assured that everything will be okay.

The nurses would come over and check me from time to time. It was Asr by now and the azan notification went off on my phone. I was in silence after saying the dua after the azan. I remembered the auspicious moment of dua after Asr on a Friday. I looked up and said to Allah, "Please let me come out of this safely, and I will not ask you for another child. I know my body has gone through a lot. But cure me, so they do not operate on me."

Wallahi, my husband came in and brought some fufu with hot pepper soup. I was dying to eat it, but the nurse quickly interrupted and said, "You cannot eat because you might be having surgery soon."

I smiled. My husband did not understand. Sabtiu looked at me and asked, "Why are they saying you cannot eat?"

I did not want him to be worried, so I said, "They said I will be able to eat later, but not now." I told him, "I can't wait to eat." It smelled so good.

Once he said he cooked it with Farhya, I knew it would taste just as expected. He was looking tired and exhausted. He hugged me, and I asked him to leave so he could be with the boys at home.

"I will be fine," I said. "I will call you if I need anything." I knew this surgery wouldn't happen.

It was as though Allah was testing me in different degrees. The evening shift had started, and my midwife said goodbye. She said, "The evening team will decide if the surgery is needed or not."

I smiled.

She said, "You are such a strong woman. Your body has gone through so much. This is the biggest baby I have delivered naturally this year. We are here to save you. If you continue bleeding like this, we will lose you. To save you, we might have to take your uterus out. I know it is hard, but please stay strong."

I smiled and thanked her.

All I did was keep asking Allah not to let this happen. I asked Allah to cure me, and I would not ask for another baby. Allah had seen me through this fatal condition (Hyperemesis Gravidarum). Some women do not make it. *I made it, and my baby is perfect, alhamdulillah*, I thought.

Not too long later, the evening team came. There was a man among them. He was quickly asked to leave, as I clearly told every one of the nurses and midwives that I want to be cared for by *only women.* He left, and the head nurse checked me. I asked the team to leave. "I do not need a crowd at my bed," I said, "just one person please."

She said, "Okay" and took care of me. She checked and said, "The bleeding is under control now."

"*Alhamdulillah*" was all I said. I was so happy. I did not need surgery anymore. Allah has answered my dua. I felt so relieved.

Life as a new mom started shortly thereafter. I experienced the same lack of sleep and tiredness and people visiting and not letting you sleep. My sincere advice is this: *When you visit a new mom, please make it brief. You do not know what she is going through. She really needs that sleep. Also, when you go visit and you are told that she is asleep, please just come back another time. Do not let anyone wake her up! She won't get that sleep she missed again. That sleep is priceless.*

I went for my postpartum visit, and my midwife congratulated me again. She made some recommendations and what broke me was when she said, "It will be fatal if you try to have another baby. From what happened last time, if it happens again, there is a high chance we would lose you or the baby."

I said, "Do not worry. God willing, this is my last baby." Then I remembered the dua I made that Friday asking Allah to save my life and if He did, I would not ask Him for another baby. *Allahu Akbar!* It was as if Allah directed her to say that to me to remind me of what I'd said. *Allahu Akbar!*

48

My Advice and Reflections

You never know what someone's situation is. Do not go around asking people when they will be having a child. It is not in their hands. Allah decides. I have always dreamed of having ten kids. *Alhamdulillah*, I have three. I can either moan and complain about the seven more I might not have, or I can look at the three I have, and thank Allah for them and the gift of my life. I chose the latter.

I am enjoying each day and thanking Allah for the blessing of children. I have had three difficult pregnancies, and I could have died; but Allah spared my life, *alhamdulillah.*

To the sister who has no child and wants a child: *May Allah bless you with children that will be the coolness of your eyes.* In the meantime, realize that children are a test. The lack of children is also a test. We are struggling to bring them up right to please Allah. Sometimes they do not listen. Sometimes they stop us from voluntary worship. They are a test. It is our sincere prayer that Allah makes this journey a fruitful one and a blessed one for us all.

To those who have children, it is not your smartness or awesomeness that gave you a child. It is by the mercy of Allah that you have a child. Don't go around making other sisters feel bad because they have no children or have less than you expect. How many people see you and ask you, "What are you waiting for?" or "Won't you have any more kids?" You do not know my journey. You do not know my pain. This is my pregnancy journey.

Taqwa, are you still there? I am still here. Earlier, I shared a little teaser about how you came to the world. You know, there is so much I want to teach you and do with you. I do not even know where to start.

From your early months, you'd enter the house copying me. Once I take off my niqab and my jilbab, you follow suit. You have become so used to the routine. You start taking off your headscarf once the door is shut behind us, as we walk into the house. I smile anytime you do that.

You know, Mommy does not know how to put on makeup. Daddy loves me looking natural. He calls it natural beauty. My mom did not put on makeup either. I grew up seeing her natural beauty blossom in front of my dad. But if you want to put on makeup, you can, and I will learn with you. We can only put it on at home, not outside. Outside the house, you need to cover up fully like the believing woman Allah talks about in the Qur'an. You are a righteous girl, and I want you to grow up even more righteous.

The world would tell you to put on makeup. I say, *No! You do not need makeup.* You are perfect, just the way you are. You need to be a servant that wakes up to worship the Lord of the worlds. You see all the billboards and ads that show these flawless looking women? They mostly need plastic surgery or some photoshop or lots of makeup to look the way you do. You are perfect, flawless, amazing, and fabulous just the way you are!

This world is not what it looks like. There is a lot of deception and lies going on. Do not be fooled by whatever you see or hear. Surround yourself with righteous friends and good company. Be with friends that remind you of Allah. Be that friend that reminds others of Allah. Be good, chaste, pure, and righteous.

You will grow up and hit puberty. It is a very unstable stage of life. You will be attracted to the opposite sex, and that is okay. That just means you are human and have hormones that are working. However, what is not okay is to be sneaky and dodgy about it. Let us sit and talk, and I will guide you through this. You will want to dress to impress. You will want to dress to stand out. Your looks will mean everything to you. That is normal.

Do you know what is not normal? To misuse this prime stage to mess up. The day you open your legs for any man other than your husband is the day you *throw your dignity* away. A virgin is a good, pure, honorable person. Society and school will tell you it is not a big deal to lose your virginity. Fornication is a *major sin* in Islam. Do not go close to it.

When your hormones are all over the place, fast. Fast as many days as you can, for it will quench this desire. Keep yourself busy with activities in the masjid and community, and it will take your mind away from the cloudy thoughts. If you are sixteen and you think you want to get married because you cannot resist the temptation, we will get you married.

Come and let us have a talk. Scared to talk to me? Then go to your dad. Still don't want to talk to him? Then go to your aunt or a sister in the community you can talk to. I know these talks might sound strange or weird to discuss with us but remember that we are here to listen. We are here to guide you through this self-defining stage in life. We are here to advise when needed and to just listen when you need us to listen.

Oh my daughter, my fears of the world and its tests and trials heightened with your birth. There is so much noise out there. It makes me fear for you. There will be lots of tests and trials out there. Remember to hold onto the Book of Allah and remain steadfast. Worship your Lord, Allah, for He is the Only One worthy of worship.

Know that your Lord, Allah, sent prophets to guide us. These prophets came with a message in the form of revelation. These revelations are our guidelines and roadmap to worship Allah. Know that we will go back to Allah and be answerable for all we did. All our deeds would be accounted for, and Allah sees you wherever you are.

This world will tell you a lot of misinformation. The Qur'an is the complete truth. It is the only revelation that has been preserved because Allah promised to preserve it. Know that the Sunnah (actions or ways of the Prophet, *sallallaahu'alayhi wa sallam*) gives us further understanding of the Qur'an. These two should be enough for you.

Beware of false prophets. For the last and seal of them all is our Prophet Muhammad (*sallallaahu'alayhi wa sallam*). Anyone who comes at your time and says he is a prophet is a *liar*. In fact, anyone who comes from now till the end of time and calls himself a prophet is a liar. There will be no other prophet. Dajjal (who is often referred to as the false Messiah or "anti-Christ") will come and Prophet Isa (Jesus, peace be upon him) will kill him after Dajjal's fatal tenure on earth. Know that Dajjal is among the major signs of the Day of Judgement. The followers of Dajjal will be a lot of women. Stay away from false trends and blind following.

Dajjal will deceive mankind in different ways. He will have the letters "*Ka-fa-ra*" on his forehead. He will claim to be God. Your God is Allah. Your God is not deficient. Dajjal will be deficient in one eye. Dajjal will promise mankind his Jannah (Paradise), which is in fact the

Hellfire. Dajjal will promise the believers his hellfire which is in fact Jannah (Paradise). If you hear of his coming, run and save yourself and your progeny. Hold onto the Qur'an. Always recite Suratul Kahf on Jumu'ah day for protection from Dajjal. Also recite the dua against Dajjal after your last *tashahud* in Salah.

Beware, Oh my child, to choose the "hellfire" of Dajjal if you encounter him. For in as much as it looks scary and fiery, that is Jannah. You will find coolness in it if he should toss you in it. It will be the greatest trial to befall mankind. I pray that Allah protects us all and the Muslims from the tests and trials of the Dajjal, *Allahuma Ameen.*

You will grow up and get married. I want you to be the best wife on earth. Work hard and strive always to gain the pleasure of Allah. Obey and respect your husband. Cherish and love him. Dress up and look good for your husband. Smell good and be a loving wife. Protect your husband's privacy and keep his home well in his absence. Do not invite to your home anyone that your husband dislikes, even if it is from your family.

Know that Allah will ask you about your duties as a wife. When you become a mother, be the best mother you can be. It is not your duty to provide for the family. It is the duty of your husband. Do not rush to work outside of the home. Your primary focus should be nurturing the home and your children. Bring them up right. Nurture and teach them what is right from wrong. Teach them how to recite the Qur'an and teach them the etiquettes and manners in Islam. Learn and teach them the hadiths.

Do not fall for the rat race of neglecting your children and going to work. Yes, a lot of people might do it, but you do not do it. You will regret when you neglect them for worldly gains. Yes, you can have a business or pursue whatever you want to do, but your children should always be your priority. Everything else can be compromised and done later, but not your *children.*

Do not fall into the nonsense of some women who say, "I will wait to accomplish my career goals before becoming a mother." *No!* Motherhood is priceless and enjoyable. Yes, it is hard work and dedication, but do not put it on hold because of a career. You can be a mother and pursue your career too. The ultimate gift you can give your children is your presence and quality time. Once you lose that, you cannot get it back.

Be there for your children. Be there for each milestone. Be there to feed them. Be there to change their diapers. Be there to give them hugs and kisses. Be there to teach them about Allah and the Prophets. Be there to sing *nasheeds* to them. Be there to teach them poetry. Be present. Be a loving mother.

When you are pregnant, be merciful to yourself. It is okay to not be able to manage yourself and the home in this stage. Reach out for help when you need it. Do not shy away. I pray to Allah that you are not tested with Hyperemesis Gravidarum. It is a rare condition that affects about 2% of pregnant women. It is rare and tough. If Allah tests you with it, know that I was tested too. Grandma was tested as well.

You will go through a lot. You will almost lose hope that it will ever get better. It really does get better. You will do several tests and your midwives will not know what to tell you at some point. Follow your instinct. If you feel like sleeping, sleep. Whatever you can eat, eat it. Remember the immense reward that awaits you.

If you need to cry, *cry*. I cried a lot. I really cried. If I am alive, I would love to help. If I am dead by then, reach out to other mothers who care and love you like their own. It will test your patience, and it will test your marriage. Please be patient. If you have nothing good to say, just cry and be quiet. Get a journal and write it all down. It is like your safe escape to release everything you are feeling. I pray that Allah, *'Azza Wa Jall*, gives you peaceful and smooth pregnancies. Enjoy motherhood, for time flies by very fast.

Breastfeed your children. Allah blessed you with those golds on your chest for a reason. Feed that baby with the priceless gift from Allah. Make sure that you are present in your children's lives in the early stages especially. Do not ship them to be looked after by someone. The only time they should be away from you is to seek knowledge and that is when they are grown, unless you want to move together with them.

Do not let someone else raise your child. It is your duty. I would love to help if I am around; but it is your duty to nurture and take care of your own children. *May Allah make marriage life, pregnancy and parenting easy for you, Allahumma Ameen.*

In the end, I love you more than life itself, and you know that. I would go through what I went through all over again just to have a daughter like you again. Death is true, and it will come. It is the destroyer of all pleasures. I will go, or you will go. We will depart from each other whether we like it or not.

Please make dua for me when I pass on. Please do not forget about me. I will do the same for you. *May Allah reunite us in Jannatul Firdaus, Allahuma Ameen.* There, we will live forever!!!

49

Dear Soldiers

Dear soldiers,

It is with much joy that I tell you this. Since you soldiers came to the world, you have been my sunshine. I wake up every morning to your smiles and hugs. I listen to all your dreams and remind you to say your morning *duas* sometimes.

You have shown me so much love, no one can compare with that. I pray that you grow up to be better than I envision for you.

You see, this life is full of tests. There will be trials and tribulations that will hit you from all corners. Allah is going to test you. But always remember that after every hardship comes ease. Sometimes you will think you cannot make it. It is in that dying moment that you should put your head down in prostration for help from The Most-High, Allah.

Remember, oh my boys, that Allah is ONE. He has no father, no mother, no son, no wife. He is *the only ONE worthy of worship.* Allah sent His messengers and prophets to show us the guidance and roadmap to worship Allah as He deserves to be worshipped. The last of these messengers is our beloved, Prophet Muhammad, *sallallaahu'alayhi wa sallam.*

All prophets came with one message and the last and complete message is the Al-Qur'an. All the other books and messages got distorted over time. The Qur'an is the only Book that is intact and complete. Allah has promised to preserve it. The Quran gives you guidelines as to how to live your lives in the service of Allah. After you die, there is an afterlife, where you will account for all you did. Please be conscious of Allah wherever you are.

The last and seal of all prophets is Muhammad, *sallallaahu'alayhi wa sallam.* Beware, Oh my soldiers, that a man called Dajjal will appear. There are so many false narrations out there about him, so the basic thing you need to remember is that he is a false prophet. He will come and disguise himself as a prophet and then later claim to be God. We have been warned about him severely by our Prophet Muhammad, *sallallaahu'alayhi wa sallam.* Recite Suratul Kahf every Jumu'ah and ponder over its meaning. Please say the dua for protection from Allah against him after your last *tashahud* in every Salah you pray. Please know that the coming of Dajjal will be a very difficult and trying time for the believers.

Hold onto the Book of Allah. No matter how strong your *emaan* is, please do not go out to see him when you hear of his arrival. Dajjal will have lots of followers, but please do not be deceived. He is the master deceiver. He will come at a time when the world is full of deception. Truth will be seen as false, and falsehood will be seen as truth. Protect yourself and your families from him. If you happen to have an encounter with him, please do not listen to him regardless of the miracles he shows you. Allah will give him the ability to show people so many miracles. *Please be strong! Be strong! Be strong!*

When Dajjal shows you his fire, choose that. For indeed, that will be Jannah (Paradise). If he entices you with his Jannah, then know that it is the fire, for everything he says is deception. But remember, fear Allah more than you fear Dajjal. Dajjal is a creation of Allah to test mankind. Hold onto your *emaan* and call upon Allah for assistance. I pray that Allah protects you all and the believers in this time from the trials of Dajjal, and grant victory to the believers, *Allahuma Ameen.*

50

Life Lessons for My Soldiers

You will live an amazing life by the will of Allah. You are going to have friends. Please choose your friends wisely. Remember that a person is on the religion of his friends. The biggest sin is *shirk*, ascribing partners to Allah, so stay away from that. Do not engage yourselves into all the "isms" that will crop up. There are a lot of ideologies out there. Stay away from them. Hold onto the Quran and the authentic hadith (sunnahs) and you will be victorious.

You will have some friends and family that would betray you. Forgive them, but do not forget so you can be careful moving forward. When you can forgive and forget, then that is better. Always try to forgive and let it go. Learn a lesson from it and move on. Try as much as possible not to hold grudges against anyone. When they hurt you, let them know that in the best way possible.

If you have nothing good to say, then be silent. You will regret saying a word that hurts someone, and they might forgive you, but you cannot take what you said back. You will never regret staying silent when you have nothing good to say.

When it is time for you to get married, please marry righteous women. Marry women who are truthful and fear Allah the most. If they are righteous and beautiful, even better. Do not let beauty blind you and tempt you to choose the wrong person. Beauty without religion is in vain. Beauty diminishes while religion and good character increases.

Be good to your wives and treat them well. Remember that they are someone's daughters whom you took in the name of Allah to protect and cherish. Remember that the Prophet Muhammad, *sallallaahu'alayhi wa sallam*, said, "The best of you are the ones that are best to their families, and I am the best to my family." Let your family see the best in you. Treat them with kind treatment.

Be there for your wife when she is pregnant. Pregnancy is very difficult. Do not run away and always be outside when she needs you and your help at home. Do not look down on her or make her cry. Yes, it is unbearable to live with pregnant women sometimes. They cry, they nag, and they have mood swings. Remember that your wife would want nothing more than order too. She is suffering more than you are because she is carrying the child. She is having the sleepless nights. She is peeing nine times in one night. She is throwing up about eight times a day, and the list continues.

Do not bring your friends around when she is pregnant or force her to cook regularly. Please be mindful of her situation and reduce visits depending on her mood. Be understanding and be empathetic. Most men do not understand this. When your wife becomes a mother, allow her to be a *mother*. She is not going to do whatever you saw me do. She is also not going to do what other mothers do sometimes. She knows what is best for her child, for the most part.

Whenever your wife needs help and advice, help her out and act as needed. Do not bring unnecessary people around giving her advice here and there and dictating to her what she should do. The first month with a newborn should be stress-free. It is hectic as it is. Do not wake her up for visits since she needs that sleep. Whoever comes around and she is asleep should come another time. That sleep is something she needs to be able to function.

Some African men are distant and not affectionate. Do not be like that. Be the man you would want to see your daughter marry. Be present in your children's lives. Most African fathers are not, and they wonder why their daughters sometimes tell them they want to marry non-African men. They are not seeing many good examples. Be a role model for your kids. Your actions speak louder than your words. They watch everything you do, so be careful.

When you become fathers, treat your children with love and respect. Do not favor one over the other. Tell your children you love them every day and spend quality time with your family. Do not live your married life like you are single. You must empathize with your wives and help them out when you can.

Dear soldiers, it does not diminish your manhood to assist at home. It makes you special and thoughtful to your wife. Do not ignore the small things that your wife does for you. Appreciate her for taking care of the home. Appreciate her for making you food to eat. Appreciate her for taking care of your kids.

Look good for your wives. It does not speak well of you to want your wives to look good for you, but you do not look good for her. Smell nice and be romantic. Give her a kiss in front of your children sometimes. Hug her and make her feel wanted. Wish her the best and be her biggest fan when she needs support.

Do not push her to work. That is not her duty. It is your duty to take care of the family. Allah put you in charge for this. You go out and work hard to provide for your family. And do not ever think you are doing your wives a favor by doing this. *No!* This is your responsibility from Allah to your wives. Even if she works, her money is for her.

Treat your wife kindly and be merciful. Have your wife in mind when you shop. Every time you shop for yourself, try to get her something too. It is not how expensive the gift is that will make her happy. It is the thoughtfulness that counts.

Educate your wives and get educated yourselves. Do not ever be satisfied with how much you know. She can learn online or in person, even if it is one day a week. Do not slack in your religion. Stay firm and upright. I do not care how many degrees you will get or earn. My primary concern is that you stay on the straight path. Hold onto your religion, and do not give it up for anything.

I would be pleased in my grave even if you are homeless and Muslim, but I would be shattered and disappointed if you are the best professor but without Islam. Learn your religion from uncorrupted people and encourage your wives to be around righteous sisters. Allah will ask you about your wives, so make sure they are good and check in from time to time.

Marry good, upright women because they will reflect what your children will be like. If you want good children, then marry good women. Remember that the mother is the first school of your child. Marry women that you are pleased with. Marry women that are nurturing and feminine. Marry women that are loving. When a woman fears Allah, she will take care of your home in your absence. She will make sure your children's *deen* and knowledge are protected and nurtured. She will not cause you pain and turmoil. She will encourage you to spend in the cause of Allah. She will be a source of peace and tranquility for you.

The right spouse is very important. May Allah, *Subhanana Wa Ta'alah*, grant you righteous spouses that will be the coolness of your eyes, and that will walk with you in Jannatul Firdaus (the highest level of Paradise) together with your lineage, *Allahuma Ameen.*

51

To My Soldiers with Love

Know that your parents are very important. Allah says what has been translated to mean, "Worship none but Allah [alone], and be dutiful to your parents" (*Al-Baqarah*, 2:83). Do not mistreat us, and do not shout at us. If we attain old age and become annoying, please be patient with us. I bore you in pain and severe pain. I spent lots of sleepless nights making sure you were okay. I cried when you were in pain, and I stayed up all night when you were sick, caring for you and making dua for you. Please treat me well.

Your dad has worked so hard to provide for us. I have never had to worry about bills. From rent to phone bills, to utility bills to your clothing, curtains, everything; he pays for them all. I want you to respect him and honor him. He had to work two jobs sometimes to provide for us. You grew up having everything. Yes, we do not buy you name brands because we are a simple family. However, you wear the best of clothes, shoes, and jackets. He makes sure your Eid outfits are paid for, your Eid gifts are paid for, your Quran completion gifts are provided for and everything. *Respect him*, as he deserves to be respected.

When you hurt others, apologize. You are going to step on people's toes, so ask for their forgiveness. Make sure you ask for your wife's forgiveness from time to time. She is your partner and the one who knows you best. You will hurt her knowingly or unknowingly. Make sure you are on a good slate with her all the time. You are going to argue, fight, have misunderstandings, but be quick to apologize when you are in the wrong. That does not make you less of a man. That makes you a *real man*.

Apologize to your children when you hurt them. I know it is not an African thing to do, but it is an *Islamic thing* to do. Whenever Islam and culture clashes, we toss culture in the garbage and hold onto what Islam says.

Do not stress your wives and families to please your friends. Your wives are your partners and not slaves to serve your family. Your wife is there to support and complement you. She is not there to take care of your family. If she wants to do that, then *alhamdulillah*. But know that, it is not her duty, nor does it make her less of a wife when she does not serve your family. I know our African culture likes to dominate and stress the wife out. That is not Islam.

When your dad and I become old, please help us as much as you can. It is not your wife's duty to assist us. If she wants to do it out of love and respect, then we would honor it. Take care of your homes. Be mindful of what your wives and children are up to. Do not be neglectful fathers who are running around with friends and have no clue what is happening in their homes.

Teach your children and share stories with them. They will remember these stories and cherish every moment you spent with them. Once you become a parent, you need to sacrifice a lot. You cannot be running out of the house because the children are bothering you. You have to man up, and deal with it. Your wife will get tired of doing everything and that would affect your marriage. Be there and help out when you can.

Teach your children the Book of Allah, Al-Quran. Share the stories of the *sahaabah* (prophetic companions) with them. Share the hadith and let them learn from righteous people. Encourage them to be in good company. That starts from you. Have good and righteous people around you. Do not let corrupt people visit your home. Do not let people who curse or use foul language into your homes. Your children should see you with good people and they would be with good people *inshaaAllah.*

No matter how much knowledge you have, respect the *scholars, imams and ustazs.* You will always be the student even if you come out better than the Ustaz that taught you *alif, baa, taa.* Humble yourself and respect the elderly. Have mercy on children and keep peace with your family members, close or far.

Life is a long journey. I cannot tell you everything about life because I am still going through it. What I can say is this: *Be strong and steadfast.* Remember, you are the children of the *lioness of Islam*.

I love you more than life itself. However, a time will come that I will be no more. Either you go before me, or I go before you. Such is the life of this world. However, the life of the Hereafter is *forever.* That is why we must work hard to please Allah and get there, Jannatul Firdaus.

Let us meet in Jannatul Firdaus where we can live happily ever after. In Jannah, there is no death. This is the time to pray our Salah, so it goes into our account of good deeds to earn us Jannah. Hold onto your Salah. Be firm in praying it on time. Live Islam and by the will of Allah, we will be reunited in Jannatul Firdaus. We will party a lot in Jannah and the party never ends. That is the party I want to go to…the one that never ends!

Love always,

Mommy

ABOUT THE AUTHOR

Mariam Elias is an African immigrant to the United States from Nima, Accra, Ghana. She is a full-time wife and a mother of three beautiful children. Her unconditional love for children comes from her own commitment to her children. She is a youth counselor and a volunteer to several immigrant families and communities in New York City.

Mariam holds a bachelor's degree in Business Administration from Ghana's Premier Private University, Valley View University, a Diploma in Islamic Studies, and a Certificate in Education from International Open University, a Certificate in Everyday Parenting from Yale University, and is pursuing a Master's degree in Public Administration at Baruch College.

She also holds several parental engagement positions and is a strong youth and children advocate. She hopes that this book brings the African Muslim community joy, answers some burning questions, and gives reassurance to others so that they know they are not alone in the challenges they face. Finally, she hopes that *Facing Life As the Girl from Nima* will spread a message of compassion and inspiration and serve as a legacy to the African immigrant community.

ACKNOWLEDGEMENTS

I would like to thank my **beloved children**, whose love for their mother is incomparable. The joy and happiness on their faces' when I told them I was writing a book was priceless.

Special thanks go to my beloved husband, **Sabtiu,** who has been my rock, my fighting mate, and my biggest fan. He has supported me from the day I dreamed of writing this book until the very last word. His love, support and encouragement are unmatched.

I also want to thank **Na'ima B. Robert** for her immense support of starting me on the writing journey. My utmost appreciation goes to **Umm Zakiyyah** who helped me with editing, and all my sisters whom I call my tribe.

My parents were my source of strength in publishing this book to the world. I say, thank you for being amazing parents.

Final thanks go to my siblings, my sisters, my tribe, and you, for choosing to read about my journey.

Thank you with love!

www.ingramcontent.com/pod-product-compliance
Ingram Content Group UK Ltd.
Pitfield, Milton Keynes, MK11 3LW, UK
UKHW041633190726
13854UKWH00006B/2475